Light Desserts

Light Desserts

The Low Calorie, Low Salt, Low Fat Way

by Deborah Kidushim-Allen

Illustrations by Heather Preston
Photographs by Hans Albers

1817

Harper & Row, Publishers, San Francisco
Cambridge, Hagerstown, New York, Philadelphia
London, Mexico City, São Paulo, Sydney

Acknowledgments

To Art, my supportive, understanding, very patient husband, and dessert devotee.

Special thanks and great appreciation go to Hans Albers for creating the beautiful photographs, to the talented Edena Sheldon for her amazing food-styling ability, and to Kathy DeKarr for her generous help in testing these recipes. For their support and help I want to thank my family and friends, especially my mother, Sarah Kidushim.

Accessories used in the photographs are from Geary's of Beverly Hills.

Light Desserts: The Low Calorie, Low Salt, Low Fat Way. Copyright © 1981 by Deborah Kidushim-Allen. All rights reserved. Printed in the United States of America. No part of this book may be used or reproduced in any manner whatsoever without written permission except in the case of brief quotations embodied in critical articles and reviews. For information address Harper & Row, Publishers, Inc., 10 East 53rd Street, New York, NY 10022. Published simultaneously in Canada by Fitzhenry & Whiteside, Limited, Toronto.

FIRST EDITION

Library of Congress Cataloging in Publication Data

Kidushim-Allen, Deborah.
    Light desserts.

    Includes index.
    1. Desserts. 2. Low-calorie diet — Recipes. 3. Salt-free diet — Recipes.
4. Low-fat diet — Recipes.
                641.8'6   81-47418
        86-X   AACR2

        84   85   10   9   8   7   6   5   4   3   2   1

Contents

Introduction

Light Desserts are desserts you deserve, desserts without guilt.

If you are a person who loves desserts, but wants to be thin and healthy too, you are in luck. As a co-author of *Light Style: The New American Cuisine*, I joined with others to develop a guide to recipe modification and menu planning that gave readers the key to eating fewer calories and less salt, fat, and sugar. Now with *Light Desserts* I show you how you can have your cake and eat it, too.

It's all here—the glamour, the delicious flavor: Poached Pears in Chocolate Sauce and Bananas Flambé, Oranges in Grand Marnier and Strawberries Romanoff Supreme, a rich chocolate soufflé and velvety ice cream bombes, Baklava and an array of fresh fruit mousses. Even those long-proscribed dieters' desserts, éclairs and cream puffs, make an appearance, the latter filled with a low-calorie, low-cholesterol vanilla ice cream (that I show you how to make) and topped with a rich chocolate sauce and almonds. You can snack, guilt free, on chewy cookies, or enjoy a number of glazed fruit tarts—raspberry, strawberry, apricot, peach, nectarine, and kiwi. Try my old-fashioned ice creams and sherbets, savarin laced with apricot sauce and crowned with blueberries, or feather-light Bavarian Mocha Cream. All that's missing are the extra calories, salt, fat, and cholesterol.

I'll show you how to make a luscious three-layer Strawberry Mousse Torte with only 141 calories per serving and very little salt, fat, and cholesterol. It is made with meringue shells of fructose and egg whites, a homemade whipped topping, strawberry nectar, a basket of fresh strawberries, and a shimmering glaze. Or maybe you are in the mood for Lemon Cheesecake. It has the same rich taste and creamy texture of New York cheesecake, but only one-third the cholesterol and 300 less calories per serving. How is it possible? You trade calorie-laden cream cheese for low-fat ricotta cheese and lemon yogurt.

Impress your family and friends with Hot Fresh Blueberry Soufflé. Start with a basket of blueberries. Then just add lemon juice, fructose, and egg substitute (contains no cholesterol and half the calories of eggs), and you have a sumptuous dessert at 115 calories, little salt, and zero fat and cholesterol per serving.

In developing these recipes, I eliminated the extra calories, salt, fat, and cholesterol wherever possible. Fruits, fruit juices, liqueurs, wines, and fructose were used as sweeteners to reduce calories. Fructose, a natural sugar made from fruits and vegetables, is much sweeter than refined sugar, therefore you need only half to two-thirds as much. Low-calorie unsalted or regular margarine was used in place of butter, egg whites or egg substitute replaced eggs, low-fat yogurt and evaporated nonfat milk were substituted for cream, beaten egg whites were used to create a creamy, fluffy texture, and salt was never added to any recipe. The goal was to modify traditional recipes not only for lower calories, salt, fat, and cholesterol, but also to increase the nutritional value as well. Yet the sinfully rich flavor and taste of these desserts belie their simple, slimming ingredients.

Many of the recipes included use fruits, because fruits are naturally low in calories, salt, fat, and cholesterol, and extra high in vitamin C and vitamin A, in addition to fiber and many needed minerals. Fruits are also naturally sweetened by nature, which helps keep extra calories out.

Cakes, cookies, tarts, ice creams, mousses, soufflés, and other satisfying desserts of every description are all here and they are all allowed. If you are skeptical, check the calorie, sodium, fat, and cholesterol information provided with each recipe. In every case, one serving is low enough to comfortably fit into a weight-reducing plan of 1,200 calories.

Desserts fill a definite need in a weight reduction or other diet program by making low-calorie needs seem complete and satisfying. *Light Desserts* combines flavor, variety, and nutrition with a gourmet touch. With this book you will not only widen your dessert repertoire, but also learn how to apply the Light Style principles to your own favorite recipes once you have worked with these.

THE RECIPES

The 150 desserts, toppings, and specialty recipes are not only lower in calories, salt, fat and cholesterol, but also, wherever possible, have higher nutritional value. In addition, recipe instructions include suggestions for adjusting ingredients to suit individual dietary needs. All the recipes have been tested several times. They have been prepared by experienced chefs and by both inexperienced and average home cooks. I have given them a final home test to make sure that instructions are accurate and easy to follow.

I have included both elegant and everyday desserts. Nutritional information with a complete nutrient breakdown per serving for calories, salt, fat, cholesterol, protein, and carbohydrate content is included with each recipe. The calculations are based on nutrient values found in authoritative sources: "Composition of Foods," Agriculture Handbooks No. 8 and 456 (Agriculture Research Service, USDA), *Food Values of Portions Commonly Used*, Bowes and Church (J. B. Lippincott Company). The nutrient analyses were calculated by a computer service, Omnihealth, Inc., to assure accuracy. All nutrient analyses following each recipe are based on the ingredients listed. When more than one choice is listed, the analysis is based on the first choice. For instance, a recipe calling for "egg substitute or eggs" will contain the nutrient analysis for egg substitute. Check the Nutrient Counter (page 171) if you wish to adjust the nutrient count to the second choice ingredient.

Most of the recipes contain about 50 percent less the amount of fat, salt, and cholesterol found in comparable traditional versions of the desserts. All have been adapted for success with the most basic home kitchen equipment.

SMALL SECRETS FOR GREAT DESSERTS

It is important that desserts please the eye as well as the palate, and my guide to baking and decorating equipment ensures beautiful as well as delectable results.

CALORIE-, SALT-, FAT-, AND CHOLESTEROL-SAVING TIPS

This section shows how to modify your favorite recipes to decrease the sugar, salt, fat, and cholesterol content.

SPECIAL PRODUCTS

In this section, I have given brand names of products used in the book, with brief descriptions of the products and where to find them. Convenience products that can be substituted for recipes in this book are also listed.

TABLE OF SUBSTITUTIONS AND EQUIVALENTS

This chart lists the equivalent measures for artificial and natural sweeteners and other commonly used ingredients for quick and easy reference.

METRIC MEASURE CONVERSION TABLES

Tables of liquid and solid measures are provided in both standard and metric units to aid you in making conversions.

NUTRIENT COUNTER

The Nutrient Counter lists calories, sodium, fat, protein, carbohydrate, and cholesterol content in household measures of commonly used foods.

Fruit Desserts

PEACH MELBA

3 large or 6 small ripe fresh freestone peaches, or
    12 unsweetened frozen and thawed or water-
    packed canned peach halves, drained
1½ cups peach nectar
1 tablespoon Kirsch
½ cup fresh or unsweetened frozen and thawed
    raspberries, or 6 tablespoons Raspberry
    Sauce (page 141)
1 tablespoon fructose (optional)
1½ cups Easy Vanilla Ice Cream (page 120) or
    low-fat vanilla yogurt
2 tablespoons toasted flaked almonds
    for garnish (optional)

Immerse the fresh peaches in a bowl of boiling water, let stand for 30 seconds, remove, peel, halve, and pit. In a medium saucepan, bring the peach nectar to a boil and cook for 2 minutes. Stir in the Kirsch, add the peach halves, lower the heat, and poach the peaches for 5 minutes. Remove from the heat and let the peaches cool in the nectar mixture.

Purée the raspberries in a food processor or blender, adding the fructose only if they need to be sweetened. Put the puréed raspberries in a saucepan and cook for 5 minutes over medium heat. Strain through a sieve and set aside to cool to room temperature.

Assemble the dessert in 6 individual fruit dishes. Put ¼ cup of ice cream in each dish. With a slotted spoon, lift the peach halves from the nectar, and place 1 or 2 on top of each serving of ice cream. Pour 1 tablespoon of the raspberry purée over each and top with 1 teaspoon of the almonds, if desired. Makes 6 servings.

NOTE: Strawberries (hulled) or nectarines (prepare as you would peaches) can be used instead of peaches.

Each serving contains about:
    67 calories
    20 mg sodium
    0 fat
    2 g protein
    14 g carbohydrate
    1 mg cholesterol

CARAMEL-CROWNED BAKED APPLES

6 cooking apples (Golden Delicious, Rome Beauty,
        or any variety that holds its shape when cooked)
½ lemon
1¼ cups unsweetened apple juice or apple cider,
        heated to boiling
Ground cinnamon
Ground nutmeg
2 tablespoons low-calorie unsalted margarine (page 149)
1 cinnamon stick
1 teaspoon pure vanilla extract
Several strips lemon peel
6 tablespoons low-fat apple yogurt,
        Light Whipped Topping (page 145), or
        commercial low-calorie whipped topping (optional)

Core the apples and peel them halfway down from the small end, reserving the apple skins. Arrange the apples, peeled ends up, in a 2-quart rectangular baking dish. Squeeze the juice of half a lemon over them and then place 1 tablespoon of apple juice in the cavity of each. Dust the apples generously with cinnamon and nutmeg and dot each cavity with 1 teaspoon of the margarine. Pour the remaining boiling apple juice into the baking dish. (The juice should be about ⅛ inch deep.) Add the cinnamon stick, vanilla extract, lemon peel, and reserved apple skins to the baking dish. Bake, uncovered, in a 350°F oven for 40 minutes, or until the apples are tender when pierced with a fork. Baste the apples with the dish juices every 10 minutes during the cooking period.

These apples may be served hot or cold. Set the apples on a serving dish, on individual plates, or in individual bowls. Pour the liquid from the baking dish into a small saucepan and boil rapidly until it becomes a light syrup. Strain the liquid over the apples and top each serving with 1 tablespoon of apple yogurt, if desired. Makes 6 servings.

CALORIE-SAVING TIP: Always carefully read labels before purchasing fruit juices to be sure that they are *unsweetened*. This same advice applies to the purchase of canned and frozen fruits.

Each serving contains about:
  137 calories
  9 mg sodium
  2 g fat
  1 g protein
  29 g carbohydrate
  1 mg cholesterol

BLUEBERRIES IN KAHLUA CREAM

**2 cups fresh blueberries, or 1 (10-ounce) package
    unsweetened frozen blueberries, thawed
½ cup low-fat vanilla yogurt
¼ cup Kahlúa**

Chill the blueberries and place ⅔ cup into each of 6 dessert glasses. Combine the yogurt and Kahlúa, stir until smooth, and pour over each serving. Makes 6 servings.

Each ⅔ cup serving contains about:
  77 calories
  10 mg sodium
  1 g fat
  1 g protein
  12 g carbohydrate
  2 mg cholesterol

4   Light Desserts

APRICOTINA

12 ripe fresh apricots, halved and pitted, or
    24 water-packed canned apricot halves, drained
1 cup low-fat apricot yogurt
¼ cup commercial low-sugar orange marmalade spread

Chill the apricot halves. Arrange 4 halves in each of 6 dessert glasses, alternating them with a teaspoonful of yogurt and dabs of orange spread and ending with yogurt topped by a dab of the spread. Makes 6 servings.

CALORIE-SAVING TIP: If you cannot find unsweetened canned fruits in the market, buy fruits canned in light syrup. Before using them, place in a colander and rinse with cold water.

Each serving contains about:
    80 calories
    20 mg sodium
    0 fat
    2 g protein
    17 g carbohydrate
    4 mg cholesterol

MIDDLE EASTERN PEARS

Excellent with a lamb dinner.

¼ pound prunes, pitted
1 cup water
½ cup red Bordeaux wine
1 cup pear nectar
    Juice of ½ lemon
3 small ripe fresh pears, peeled, halved, and cored, or
    6 water-packed canned pear halves, drained

Place the prunes, water, and wine in a saucepan and let stand overnight. The next day, cook the prune mixture over medium heat for a few minutes. Remove from the heat and let the prunes cool in the liquid.

In a saucepan large enough to hold the pears, combine the pear nectar and lemon juice. Slowly bring the nectar to a boil and add the pears. Cook over low heat until the pears are soft but still hold their shape, turning them frequently in the nectar as they cook. The cooking time will vary with the variety and ripeness of the fruit. Remove from the heat and let the pears cool in the liquid. Mix together the cooled prunes and pears and their cooking liquids and chill before serving. Makes 6 servings.

Each serving contains about:
   108 calories
   4 mg sodium
   0 fat
   1 g protein
   25 g carbohydrate
   0 cholesterol

NUT-BAKED APPLES WITH YOGURT-BRANDY SAUCE

Yes, you can use liqueur in diet desserts. The key is to add only a small amount to round out the flavor.

   6 cooking apples (Golden Delicious, Rome Beauty, or
       other variety that will hold its shape when cooked)
   ½ lemon
   2 tablespoons low-calorie unsalted margarine (page 149)
   3 tablespoons chopped pecans or nuts of choice
   2 tablespoons fructose
   ½ teaspoon ground cinnamon
   ¼ teaspoon ground nutmeg
   1 cup unsweetened apple juice or apple cider,
       heated to boiling
   ½ cup low-fat apple yogurt
   1 tablespoon brandy

Core the apples and peel them halfway down from the small end, reserving the apple skins. Arrange the apples, peeled ends up, in a 2-

quart rectangular baking dish. Squeeze the juice of half a lemon over them. In a small bowl, combine the margarine, nuts, fructose, cinnamon, and nutmeg and mix well. Fill the cavity of each apple with an equal amount of the mixture. Pour the boiling apple juice over the apples (the juice should be about ¼ inch deep in the dish), and add the reserved skins to the dish. Bake, uncovered, in a 350°F oven for 40 minutes, or until the apples are tender when pierced with a fork. Baste the apples with the dish juices every 10 minutes during the cooking period. Remove from the oven, let cool, and chill.

At serving time, stir together the yogurt and brandy and spoon an equal amount over each apple. Makes 6 servings.

Each serving contains about:
  174 calories
  21 mg sodium
  4 g fat
  2 g protein
  37 g carbohydrate
  4 mg cholesterol

MELON WITH PEACHES

1 medium honeydew, cantaloupe, or melon of
    choice, halved and seeded
3 medium ripe fresh freestone peaches, or
    2 cups unsweetened frozen and thawed or
    water-packed canned peach slices
3 tablespoons Rose Water Syrup (page 78)

With a melon baller, make melon balls from the honeydew. Put them in a bowl with any juice from the melon. Immerse the fresh peaches in a bowl of boiling water for 30 seconds, remove, peel, pit, and thinly slice. Add the peaches and Rose Water Syrup to the melon balls and toss lightly. Cover the bowl and refrigerate for several hours or overnight.

To serve, spoon into 6 dessert glasses. Makes 6 servings.

Each ½ cup serving contains about:
  147 calories

19 mg sodium
0 fat
2 g protein
16 g carbohydrate
0 cholesterol

PINEAPPLE MEDLEY

1 large ripe pineapple (about 3½ pounds),
    halved lengthwise
1 tablespoon fructose
2 tablespoons Kirsch or unsweetened pineapple juice
1 tablespoon plus 2 teaspoons fresh
    lemon or lime juice
1 lime, thinly sliced
2 firm ripe bananas, sliced
1 medium ripe cantaloupe, halved, seeded, peeled,
    and cut into 1-inch cubes
2 Red Delicious apples, unpeeled and sliced
Lemon leaves for garnish
2 cups unhulled whole fresh strawberries
    for garnish (optional)

With a sharp knife, remove fruit from each pineapple half, leaving a ½-inch-thick shell and being careful not to cut through the skin. Set the shells aside. Remove and discard the core from the fruit. Purée half of the pineapple in a food processor or blender for about 1 minute. Add the fructose, Kirsch, and 1 tablespoon of the lemon juice. Mix until well blended. Slice remaining pineapple into 1-inch cubes. Place the pineapple cubes, lime slices, bananas, cantaloupe, and apples in a large bowl. Add the remaining lemon juice to the fruit and toss gently. Add the pineapple purée and stir gently. Cover and marinate for 1 to 2 hours.

To serve, divide the fruit evenly among the prepared shells. Line a serving platter with lemon leaves and set the filled shells on top. Garnish with whole strawberries, if desired. Makes 12 servings.

Each ¾ cup serving contains about:
  82 calories
  7 mg sodium
  0 fat
  1 g protein
  21 g carbohydrate
  0 cholesterol

POACHED BLUEBERRIES

½ cup blueberry nectar
Juice of ½ lemon
1 strip lemon peel
1 cinnamon stick
1 whole clove
2 cups fresh blueberries, or
    1 (10-ounce) package unsweetened frozen
    blueberries, thawed
6 tablespoons Light Whipped Topping (page 145) or
    commercial low-calorie whipped topping (optional)

Bring the blueberry nectar to a boil, lower the heat, and simmer until it becomes a light syrup. Add the lemon juice and peel, cinnamon stick, and clove and simmer a few minutes. Add the blueberries and simmer several minutes until the berries are cooked but still hold their shape. Remove from the heat, let cool, cover, and refrigerate for 24 hours to allow the flavors to blend.

To serve, spoon ½ cup of the berry mixture into each of 6 sherbet glasses and top each with 1 tablespoon of whipped topping, if desired. Makes 6 servings.

Each ½ cup serving contains about:
  42 calories
  0 sodium
  0 fat
  0 protein
  10 g carbohydrate
  0 cholesterol

MINTED APRICOTS

2 tablespoons white crème de menthe
1 cup Light Whipped Topping (page 145) or
    commercial low-calorie whipped topping
12 ripe fresh apricots, halved and pitted, or
    24 water-packed canned apricot halves, drained
6 fresh mint leaves for garnish

Fold the crème de menthe into the whipped topping. Arrange 4 apricot halves in each of 6 dessert glasses. Spoon 3 tablespoons of the crème de menthe mixture over the apricots. Decorate each glass with a mint leaf. Makes 6 servings.

Each serving contains about:
    64 calories
    14 mg sodium
    1 g fat
    2 g protein
    12 g carbohydrate
    0 cholesterol

PEACHES IN PORT

¾ cup unsweetened white grape juice
1 cup dessert wine (port, muscatel, or Malaga)
6 medium ripe fresh freestone peaches, or
    12 unsweetened frozen and thawed or water-packed
    canned peach halves, drained

In a bowl, combine the grape juice and wine and stir until blended. Immerse the fresh peaches in a bowl of boiling water, let stand for 30 seconds, remove, and peel. Quarter and pit each peach. Place the peach quarters in the wine mixture, cover, and refrigerate for at least 1 hour before serving. Makes 6 servings.

Each ½ cup serving contains about:
    89 calories
    2 mg sodium
    0 fat
    1 g protein
    17 g carbohydrate
    0 cholesterol

APRICOT-POACHED APPLES
WITH ORANGE CREAM

6 apples (Golden Delicious or Rome Beauty)
Juice of ½ lemon
¾ cup water
½ cup commercial low-sugar apricot spread
1 teaspoon freshly grated orange zest
Orange Cream (following recipe)
6 fresh mint leaves for garnish

Peel and core the apples and rub them with the lemon juice. Place the apples in a skillet or saucepan wide enough to hold them in a single layer. Combine the water, apricot spread, and orange zest in a small saucepan. Bring to a boil, stirring constantly, lower the heat, and simmer for a few minutes. Pour the apricot mixture around the apples in the skillet. Cover and simmer over low heat until the apples are tender but still firm, about 30 to 40 minutes. Baste with the pan juices a few times during the cooking period. Remove the apples to a dish and let cool, then cover and refrigerate to chill thoroughly.

To serve, spoon 3 tablespoons of the Orange Cream onto each of 6 individual serving dishes. Place an apple on each bed of cream. Spoon an equal amount of the remaining Orange Cream over each apple and garnish with a mint leaf. Makes 6 servings.

Orange Cream

1½ cups low-fat orange yogurt
¼ cup unsweetened orange juice
1 teaspoon pure vanilla extract
1 tablespoon orange-flavored liqueur (optional)

Combine the yogurt, orange juice, vanilla extract, and liqueur in a small bowl and stir until well blended. Refrigerate until serving time. Makes 1¾ cups.

Each serving contains about:
131 calories
30 mg sodium
2 g fat
3 g protein
29 g carbohydrate
3 mg cholesterol

SHERRIED WATERMELON

5 cups cubed (¾ inch) seeded watermelon
½ cup sherry
½ teaspoon ground nutmeg

In a large bowl, toss together the watermelon cubes, sherry, and nutmeg. Cover and refrigerate at least 2 hours, stirring occasionally. Spoon the mixture into 6 dessert glasses. Makes 6 servings.

Each ¾ cup serving contains about:
58 calories
4 mg sodium
0 fat
0 protein
14 g carbohydrate
0 cholesterol

BANANAS FLAMBE

5 small firm, ripe, unblemished bananas, sliced
  ¼-inch thick on the diagonal
2 tablespoons low-calorie unsalted margarine (page 149)
½ cup unsweetened orange juice
2 teaspoons fresh lemon juice
One 2-inch piece cinnamon stick
2 whole cloves
3 tablespoons brandy

Arrange the banana slices in a lightly greased nonstick baking dish large enough to hold them without the slices touching. Combine the margarine, orange juice, lemon juice, cinnamon stick, cloves, and 2 tablespoons of the brandy in a small saucepan. Bring to a boil, stirring occasionally, then pour over the bananas. Bake in a 400°F oven for 15 minutes, basting occasionally with the sauce.

Remove from the oven and arrange the banana slices in a serving dish with the sauce remaining in the baking dish. Pour the remaining 1 tablespoon brandy over the bananas and ignite the brandy. When the flame dies, baste the bananas with the sauce and serve. Makes 6 servings.

CALORIE-SAVING TIP: Brandy is highly caloric. For a low-calorie substitute, use rum extract. Since all alcoholic beverages are sugar based, use them sparingly, like you would an extract. The liquors that are highest in calories are the high-proof, very sweet, and fruit-based ones. Refer to page 171 for the calorie content of various liquors.

Each serving (6 slices) contains about:
  78 calories
  1 mg sodium
  0 fat
  1 g protein
  15 g carbohydrate
  0 cholesterol

ORANGES IN GRAND MARNIER

6 medium seedless oranges (navels are best)
½ cup water
½ cup Grand Marnier
½ cup unsweetened orange juice

Using a vegetable peeler, thinly pare the peel from 1 orange. Cut the peel into needlelike strips, combine with the water in a saucepan, and boil for 5 minutes. Drain and dry on paper toweling.

Cut the peel, pith, and outer membrane from the oranges, including the one already pared, so the flesh is exposed. The best way to do this is to use a serrated-edged knife and to cut with a sawing motion to avoid losing any juice. Then, using a plate for the cutting surface, cut each orange into ¼-inch-thick slices. Reshape each orange into its original form and spear the slices together with a toothpick. Arrange the oranges in a deep glass dish. Reserve the orange juice that collected on the plate.

In a small saucepan, bring the Grand Marnier to a boil and cook steadily until it becomes a syrupy glaze. Pour in the reserved orange juice and bring back to a boil. Remove from the heat and pour on top of the oranges. Sprinkle the reserved orange peel over the top and chill before serving. Makes 6 servings.

Each serving contains about:
80 calories
2 mg sodium
0 fat
1 g protein
13 g carbohydrate
0 cholesterol

BLACKBERRY FLUMMERY

2 cups fresh blackberries
1 cup blackberry nectar
3 tablespoons plus 1 teaspoon cornstarch
1 tablespoon fresh lemon juice
1½ cups low-fat blackberry yogurt, Light Whipped
    Topping (page 145), or commercial low-calorie
    whipped topping, or 1 pint Easy Vanilla Ice
    Cream (page 120)

Combine the blackberries and nectar in a saucepan, bring to a boil, lower the heat, and simmer for about 5 minutes. Remove from the heat and press the mixture through a fine sieve or foodmill. Add enough cold water to measure 2½ cups and return the mixture to the saucepan. Combine a small amount of the blackberry mixture with the cornstarch and stir until smooth. Stir the cornstarch mixture into the blackberry mixture. Add the lemon juice and cook over medium heat, stirring constantly, until the mixture thickens. Remove from the heat, let cool, cover, and chill.

To serve, spoon the blackberry mixture into 6 dessert glasses. Top each with ¼ cup yogurt. Makes 6 servings.

Each ½ cup serving contains about:
    128 calories
    30 mg sodium
    1 g fat
    3 g protein
    27 g carbohydrate
    4 mg cholesterol

CHOCOLATE-ALMOND FIGS

18 large dried figs
⅓ cup ground toasted blanched almonds or pecans
2 tablespoons grated semisweet chocolate or carob
18 toasted whole blanched almonds or pecans

Cut the stems off the figs. Make a ½-inch-deep depression in the stem end of each with your fingertip. Mix together the ground almonds and chocolate and stuff the mixture into the figs, pinching the openings together firmly. Arrange the figs, stem ends up, on a nonstick baking sheet and bake in a 350°F oven for 10 minutes. Remove from the oven and let cool slightly. Press a whole almond gently but firmly into each fig and pinch the fig to secure the almond in place. Serve at room temperature. Makes 18 stuffed figs.

NOTE: Store the figs in a tightly covered container lined with sheets of waxed paper.

Each fig contains about:
42 calories
6 mg sodium
2 g fat
1 g protein
13 g carbohydrate
0 cholesterol

CHOCOLATE-DIPPED FRESH FRUITS

½ cup semisweet chocolate or carob chips
30 large fresh strawberries, orange segments, peach
   slices, or fruit of choice (choose perfect fruits
   with no breaks in the surface that could leak
   moisture)

In the top pan of a double boiler placed over simmering water (do not let it boil), melt the chocolate, stirring until smooth and satiny. Stirring ensures good color and quicker hardening after fruits have been dipped. Remove from the heat and dip the pieces of fruit into the chocolate to coat, holding them over the pan briefly to allow the excess chocolate to drain. Place the coated fruits on a piece of waxed paper and let stand until the chocolate has hardened. Makes 10 servings.

NOTE: Moisture is the enemy of chocolate dipping. Be sure that the fruit's surface is dry before dipping, and do not allow moisture of any kind to drip into the dipping medium. To dry very moist fruits, like oranges, place them in a sieve in a very warm, turned-off oven for 2 to 3 minutes. Do not store chocolate-dipped fruits in the refrigerator, as this causes the chocolate to turn gray and lose its sheen.

Each serving (3 pieces) contains about:
65 calories
1 mg sodium
3 g fat
1 g protein
10 g carbohydrate
0 cholesterol

POACHED PEARS IN CHOCOLATE SAUCE

6 small ripe fresh pears
Fresh lemon juice
1½ cups pear nectar
¼ cup semisweet chocolate or carob chips
1 tablespoon evaporated nonfat milk

Peel the pears under cold, running water with a vegetable peeler, leaving them whole with stems intact. Brush with lemon juice to prevent discoloration. In a large saucepan, combine the pear nectar and pears. Cook over low heat for 20 to 25 minutes, testing frequently to see if the pears are cooked. When cooked but still firm to the touch, carefully remove the pears from the juice and chill, reserving the cooking liquid.

When ready to serve, rapidly boil the cooking liquid until reduced to about ¼ cup. Add the chocolate chips and stir until the chocolate melts and the sauce is smooth. Beat the milk into the sauce with a wire whisk.

To serve, spoon about 1 tablespoon of the chocolate sauce onto each of 6 individual serving plates. Place a pear on each bed of sauce. Makes 6 servings.

Each serving contains about:
160 calories
6 mg sodium
4 g fat
1 g protein
35 g carbohydrate
0 cholesterol

FRESH RASPBERRIES WITH
GRAND MARNIER SAUCE

1 tablespoon fructose
½ teaspoon cornstarch
½ cup strawberry nectar
 Finely grated zest of ½ orange
 Finely grated zest of ½ lemon
¼ vanilla bean, split lengthwise, or
    ½ teaspoon pure vanilla extract
½ cup egg substitute (page 150), or
    4 egg yolks, lightly beaten
1½ teaspoons unflavored gelatin, softened in
    2 tablespoons cold water
1 cup Light Whipped Topping (page 145) or
    commercial low-calorie whipped topping
1 tablespoon Mandarin Napoléon liqueur or
    orange-flavored liqueur of choice
2 tablespoons Grand Marnier
3 cups fresh, unsweetened frozen and thawed, or
    water-packed canned and drained raspberries
    or hulled strawberries

Combine the fructose and cornstarch in the top pan of a double boiler and mix well. Stir in the strawberry nectar, orange and lemon zests, and vanilla bean until well blended. Set over simmering water and stir constantly until mixture begins to thicken, about 5 minutes. Stir a small amount of the nectar mixture into the egg substitute or yolks, then add egg substitute or yolks to the pan and continue cooking, stirring constantly, until thickened, about 5 minutes. Stir in gelatin, blending thoroughly. Remove from the heat. Pour the mixture through a strainer into a large bowl. Let cool, cover, and chill.

To serve, fold the whipped topping into the chilled mixture. Add Mandarin Napoléon liqueur and Grand Marnier and stir until smooth. Arrange ½ cup raspberries in each of 6 individual dessert dishes and pour an equal amount of the sauce over each serving. Makes 6 servings.

Each ½ cup serving contains about:
   115 calories
   34 mg sodium

2 g fat
4 g protein
17 g carbohydrate
1 mg cholesterol

PEACH DAIQUIRI

For good nutrition, as well as to quench your thirst and satisfy your sweet tooth, try this nonalcoholic cocktail. Peach Daiquiri contributes a significant amount of vitamin C and vitamin A for a reasonable number of calories.

2 (16-ounce) cans water-packed peach slices or halves
¼ fresh lime juice
2 tablespoons fructose
1 teaspoon rum extract
1 cup cracked ice
Mint sprigs for garnish

Purée peaches, including juice from cans, in a food processor or blender. Freeze until firm. (This will make about 3½ cups of frozen purée.) Combine frozen purée, lime juice, fructose, rum extract, and ice in a food processor or blender. Blend for 10 seconds, or until smooth. Pour ½ cup into each of 6 chilled, long-stemmed glasses. Garnish with mint sprigs. Makes 6 servings.

NOTE: Water-packed canned pears, pineapple, or apricots may be substituted for the peaches.

Each ½ cup serving contains approximately:
67 calories
3 mg sodium
0 fat
1 g protein
18 g carbohydrate
0 cholesterol

BERRY DELIGHT

There are only three ingredients in this tangy treat!

4 small fresh peaches
1½ cups fresh blueberries
2½ tablespoons low-calorie maple syrup

Immerse the peaches in a bowl of boiling water for 30 seconds, remove, peel, pit, and slice. Place the peaches in a glass serving bowl, top with the blueberries, and sprinkle with the maple syrup. Toss before serving. Makes 6 servings.

VARIATION: Substitute 3 oranges, peeled and sectioned, for the peaches and ¼ cup unsweetened orange juice for the maple syrup. Dust with ground cinnamon just before serving.

Each ½ cup serving contains about:
58 calories
1 mg sodium
0 fat
1 g protein
14 g carbohydrate
0 cholesterol

SUNSHINE PEACH PUNCH

A frosty fruit drink for entertaining.

3½ ounces unsweetened frozen pineapple juice
**   concentrate**
1 medium ripe fresh peach, peeled and chopped, or
**   2 water-packed canned peach halves, drained**
**   and chopped**
1 tablespoon unsweetened frozen orange juice
**   concentrate**
¾ cup cold water
1 egg white
10 ice cubes
4 pineapple wedges or orange slices for garnish (optional)
Fresh mint leaves for garnish (optional)

Combine the pineapple juice concentrate, peach, orange juice concentrate, water, egg white, and ice cubes in a food processor or blender. Blend until smooth and thick. Pour ½ cup into each of 4 chilled, long-stemmed glasses and garnish with a pineapple wedge and mint leaves, if desired. Makes 6 servings.

Each ½ cup serving contains about:
    60 calories
    15 mg sodium
    0 fat
    2 g protein
    13 g carbohydrate
    0 cholesterol

FRUITS AU VIN ROUGE

1¼ cups red wine or white grape juice
¾ cup water
1 tablespoon fructose
1 vanilla bean, split lengthwise
½ pound pears
½ pound melon of choice
½ pound apricots
½ pound peaches
½ pound strawberries, hulled
½ pound cherries, pitted and left whole
Fresh mint leaves for garnish

In a saucepan, simmer the wine until it is reduced by half so that virtually all the alcohol evaporates. Add the water, fructose, and vanilla bean and bring the mixture back to a boil. Remove from the heat, cool, and refrigerate.

Over a bowl to catch the juice, peel the larger fruits, core or pit them, and cut them into half-moon slices or sections. Leave the berries and cherries whole. Combine all of the fruits and their juices and marinate for at least 1 hour in the refrigerator.

To serve, spoon the fruits and their juices into 12 chilled glasses, pour the sweetened wine over (removing the vanilla bean), and decorate with the mint leaves. Makes 12 servings.

NOTE: Any ripe fresh fruits in season or a combination of fresh and unsweetened canned or frozen fruits may be used in this dessert. It may be served in a glass bowl or in a fruit skin, such as pineapple, orange, or grapefruit. Fruits with little acid should be sprinkled with lemon juice to prevent discoloration.

CALORIE-SAVING TIP: Seasonal fresh fruit is preferable to canned or frozen, not only for the flavor, but also because sugar is generally added during processing. To eliminate the sugar added in processing, put the fruit in a sieve or colander, drain off all the liquid, and rinse in cold water. If using canned fruits, look for ones packed in water. Always choose unsweetened frozen fruits.

VARIATION: For each serving, spoon ½ cup of the prepared fruits and sauce into individual meringue shells (page 82) and garnish with fresh mint leaves.

Each ½ cup serving contains about:
    74 calories
    4 mg sodium
    0 fat
    1 g protein
    16 g carbohydrate
    0 cholesterol

Clockwise, from lower left: Glazed Summer- or Winter-Fruit Tartlets, Kiwi Tart, Strawberry Tart, Tart à l'Orange, and Light Whipped Topping.

Clockwise, from upper left: Baklava, Profiteroles in Chocolate Sauce, and assorted cookies, from left to right, Délices with Fruit (also on small plate above), Raisin-Nut Cookies, Boysenberry Bar, and, scattered around the plate, Leaf Cookies

POACHED PEARS IN ORANGE SAUCE

Pears, a wintertime gift of nature, come to the table as a smashing, sophisticated dessert—poached in vanilla-scented syrup and dressed in a shimmering mantle of spiced, brandied orange sauce.

2 tablespoons fresh lemon juice
6 medium fresh pears of uniform ripeness
1½ cups pear nectar
One 3-inch piece vanilla bean, split lengthwise
One 3-inch piece cinnamon stick
Zest of 2 oranges, cut into ⅛-inch-wide julienne
2 teaspoons cornstarch
¾ cup fresh orange juice, strained
1 cup commercial low-sugar orange marmalade spread
½ cup Cointreau, or
    ½ cup water, mixed with ½ teaspoon rum extract
2 tablespoons cognac or brandy
¼ teaspoon ground cinnamon

Stir the lemon juice into a large bowl of cold water. Peel the pears under cold, running water with a vegetable peeler, leaving them whole with stems intact. Immediately put the pears in the lemon water. Combine the pear nectar, vanilla bean, and cinnamon stick in a Dutch oven or any large heavy pot with a lid. Bring to a boil, drain and add the pears, lower the heat, and simmer until the pears are tender when pierced with the tip of a sharp knife, about 20 to 25 minutes. Transfer the pears to a medium bowl and pour the poaching liquid over them. Let cool to room temperature.

Meanwhile, blanch the orange zest in boiling water for 5 minutes, drain, and dry on paper toweling. Set aside. Mix the cornstarch with 2 tablespoons of the orange juice and set aside. Melt the orange marmalade spread over low heat in a medium saucepan until smooth and gradually stir in the remaining orange juice. Heat the mixture to boiling and cook, whisking frequently, until the sauce is reduced to 1 cup. Reduce the heat to medium and whisk in the reserved cornstarch mixture, whisking constantly until the sauce thickens and bubbles for 3 minutes. Reduce the heat to low and stir in the Cointreau and cognac. Simmer for 2 minutes and remove from the heat. Stir in the ground cinnamon. Let cool slightly, cover, and refrigerate until cooled completely but not chilled.

To serve, remove the pears from the poaching liquid and pat dry. Place a pear on each of 6 individual serving plates. Spoon the orange sauce over the pears. Garnish with the reserved orange zest. Makes 6 servings.

CALORIE-SAVING TIP: Liqueurs like Cointreau are highly caloric. Rum extract is a good low-calorie substitute. All alcohol is sugar based, so use it sparingly as you would an extract.

Each serving contains about:
186 calories
3 mg sodium
1 g fat
2 g protein
40 g carbohydrate
0 cholesterol

TANGERINES AND KIWIS

This dessert is *la nouvelle cuisine* at its most stunning.

2 oranges
2 cups white grape juice
6 large tangerines, or 4 medium oranges
5 kiwis
Fruit Sauce (following recipe)

With a vegetable peeler, remove the peels of 2 oranges in very thin strips and cut the strips into a julienne of long, thin sticks as fine as pine needles. In a saucepan, bring the grape juice to a boil, add the julienned orange peel, and simmer over very low heat for 45 minutes, or until the orange peel is coated with syrup. Remove from the heat, let cool, cover, and refrigerate.

Meanwhile, peel the tangerines completely, removing all of the white pith. Over a bowl to catch the juice (reserve the juice for the Fruit Sauce), cut out the sections of the tangerines between the membranes. (If you are using oranges instead of tangerines, remove the white pith from the 2 oranges used for preparing the julienne of orange peel and completely peel the 4 additional oranges. Section them as directed for the tangerines.) Peel the kiwis and cut them crosswise into thin slices. Chill the fruits thoroughly while preparing the Fruit Sauce.

To serve, spoon a band of chilled Fruit Sauce around the perimeter of each of 6 individual serving plates. Arrange the tangerine sections in a pinwheel in the center of eachand the kiwi slices in a ring around them. Lift the orange peel from the syrup with a slotted spoon and arrange them over the tangerines. Makes 6 servings.

Fruit Sauce

½ cup ricotta cheese (made from partially skimmed milk)
¾ cup low-fat vanilla yogurt
2 teaspoons cornstarch
¼ cup tangerine or orange juice reserved from
    preparing the sectioned fruit, strained
3 tablespoons egg substitute (page 150), or 2 egg yolks
2 tablespoons fructose

In a medium saucepan, whisk together the ricotta cheese and yogurt until smooth. Dissolve the cornstarch in the tangerine juice and whisk into the yogurt mixture. Beat the egg substitute or yolks until well blended and add the fructose, beating well. Add to the mixture in the pan. Cook over medium heat, stirring constantly, just until the mixture thickens and heavily coats a spoon. Immediately remove from the heat and transfer the mixture to a bowl. Let cool, then chill the sauce thoroughly.

Each serving contains about:
    101 calories
    20 mg sodium
    2 g fat
    6 g protein
    10 g carbohydrate
    9 mg cholesterol

BANANA CREAM

4 very ripe bananas
1 tablespoon fresh lemon juice
½ cup low-fat vanilla yogurt
1 tablespoon orange-flavored liqueur (optional)
6 long-stemmed fresh strawberries, violets, or
    lilacs for garnish

Mash the bananas, add the lemon juice and yogurt, and mix well. For a smoother texture, put the mixture in an electric blender at medium speed for 5 seconds or in a food processor for 1 second. Cover and refrigerate until chilled.

To serve, stir in liqueur, if desired, and spoon the mixture into 6 long-stemmed sherbet glasses. Garnish each with a strawberry. Makes 6 servings.

Each ½ cup serving contains approximately:
    78 calories
    11 mg sodium
    0 fat
    2 g protein
    19 g carbohydrate
    1 mg cholesterol

STRAWBERRIES ROMANOFF SUPREME

1 cup plus 3 tablespoons evaporated nonfat milk
1 envelope (1 tablespoon) unflavored gelatin
1 cup low-fat strawberry yogurt
½ teaspoon pure vanilla extract
4 cups fresh strawberries, hulled
½ cup unsweetened orange juice
2 tablespoons orange-flavored liqueur

In a saucepan, mix together the milk and gelatin and heat gently until the gelatin thoroughly dissolves. Remove from the heat and cool until slightly thickened. Fold in the yogurt and vanilla extract and whisk until the mixture is smooth. Pour the mixture into a serving bowl, a 3-cup metal mold, or 6 individual ½-cup molds. Cover and chill until set, at least 4 hours.

Meanwhile, put the strawberries in a bowl and pour the orange juice and liqueur over them. Cover and chill.

To serve, unmold the yogurt mixture by briefly dipping the container(s) into hot water almost to the rim(s). When the edges of the mixture *just begin* to liquefy, lift from the water and invert onto chilled serving plate(s). Liberally surround with the chilled strawberries. Makes 6 servings.

Each ½ cup serving contains about:
    134 calories
    45 mg sodium
    1 g fat
    7 g protein
    24 g carbohydrate
    7 mg cholesterol

STRAWBERRIES A LA CREME

30 jumbo fresh strawberries, hulled
2 tablespoons sherry, sweet marsala, cognac, rum, or
    almond- or orange-flavored liqueur
1½ cups Light Whipped Topping (page 145) or
    commercial low-calorie whipped topping

From the pointed end, split each berry into quarters, but do not cut clear through the stem end. Cover and chill thoroughly.

To serve, fold wine into whipped topping. Put the topping in a pastry bag fitted with a ½-inch star tip. Stand the chilled berries on a serving dish, pointed ends up, and generously pipe the topping into the center of each berry. Makes 6 servings.

Each serving (5 filled berries) contains about:
    68 calories
    21 mg sodium
    2 g fat
    2 g protein
    11 g carbohydrate
    0 cholesterol

MANGO CREAM

2 large ripe mangoes, peeled and chopped
2 tablespoons unsweetened orange juice
2 teaspoons fresh lemon juice
1 tablespoon fructose (optional)
2 cups Light Whipped Topping (page 145) or
   commercial low-calorie whipped topping
1 tablespoon chopped pistachio nuts or
   pecans for garnish

Purée the mangoes in a food processor or blender with the orange and lemon juices, adding the fructose if additional sweetness is desired. Transfer the mixture to a bowl and gently but thoroughly fold in the whipped topping. Cover and chill.

To serve, spoon into 6 individual serving dishes and sprinkle with chopped nuts. Makes 6 servings.

NOTE: Peaches, papayas, strawberries, bananas, or nectarines may be substituted for the mangoes.

Each ¾ cup serving contains about:
86 calories
31 mg sodium
3 g fat
3 g protein
15 g carbohydrate
0 cholesterol

Soufflés

COLD PUMPKIN SOUFFLE

½ teaspoon low-calorie margarine (page 149)
¼ cup ginger-flavored brandy
1 envelope (1 tablespoon) unflavored gelatin
½ cup egg substitute (page 150), or 4 egg yolks
¼ cup fructose
1 (16-ounce) can unsweetened pumpkin
1 teaspoon freshly grated orange zest
1 teaspoon ground cinnamon
½ teaspoon ground ginger
¼ teaspoon ground mace
¼ teaspoon ground cloves
4 egg whites, at room temperature
1 teaspoon white vinegar
1 cup Light Whipped Topping (page 145) or
    commercial low-calorie whipped topping
¼ cup chopped toasted walnuts, pecans, or
    almonds for garnish (optional)
2 tablespoons unsweetened frozen orange juice
    concentrate, thawed (optional)
1 cup Easy Vanilla Ice Cream (page 120, optional),
    slightly softened

Cut a 7-inch-wide band of waxed paper that is long enough to encircle a 1-quart soufflé dish with a 2-inch overlap. Lightly grease the waxed paper and secure it to the dish with tape, greased side in, so that it forms a 2-inch-wide collar above the rim of the dish. (Or prepare six 3-inch-wide bands of waxed paper around 6 individual soufflé dishes.) Pour the brandy into the top pan of a double boiler placed over simmering water and sprinkle in the gelatin. Stir constantly until the gelatin completely dissolves.

Combine the egg substitute or yolks and 2 tablespoons of the fructose in a medium bowl and beat until thick. Blend in the pumpkin, orange zest, cinnamon, ginger, mace, and cloves, then mix in the dissolved gelatin. Beat the egg whites at low speed until foamy. Add the vinegar and beat at medium speed until soft peaks form. Gradually adding the remaining fructose, beat at high speed until stiff, glossy peaks form. Stir one-fourth of the egg whites into the pumpkin mixture to lighten it, then gently fold in the remaining whites. Fold the whipped topping into the pumpkin mixture and spoon into the soufflé dish or dishes. Chill until set, at least 8 hours.

Carefully remove the collar(s). Decorate the soufflé(s) with a border of nuts. If desired, blend the orange juice concentrate with the ice cream and pass separately as a sauce. Makes 6 servings.

NOTE: The sodium content can be reduced by approximately 80 mg per serving by using fresh pumpkin, or canned pumpkin without added salt.

Each ½ cup serving contains about:
   121 calories
   231 mg sodium
   0 fat
   6 g protein
   17 g carbohydrate
   1 mg cholesterol

LEMON SOUFFLE IN LEMON SHELLS
WITH RASPBERRY SAUCE

   6 large lemons
   ½ cup egg substitute (page 150), or 3 egg yolks
   ½ cup fructose
   Freshly grated zest of 1 lemon
   4 egg whites, at room temperature
   1 teaspoon white vinegar
   Fresh lemon leaves for garnish
   6 tablespoons Raspberry Sauce (page 141)

Slice off both ends of each lemon so it will stand upright when set on either end. Halve crosswise either straight or in a zigzag design, making 12 lemon cups. With a grapefruit knife or teaspoon, gently remove the pulp, taking care not to pierce the skins. Squeeze and strain 3 tablespoons of juice from the pulp and set the juice aside. Drain the shells upside down on paper toweling.

Combine the egg substitute or yolks with 3 tablespoons of the fructose in a medium bowl and beat until thick. Stir in the reserved lemon juice and the zest. Beat the egg whites at low speed until foamy. Add the vinegar and beat at medium speed until soft peaks form. Gradually adding the remaining fructose, beat at high speed until stiff, glossy peaks form. Stir one-fourth of the egg whites into the egg yolk mixture to lighten it, then gently fold in the remaining whites. Evenly spoon the mixture into the 12 lemon cups. Place the lemon cups in a 9-by-13-inch shallow baking dish and bake in a 375°F oven for 15 to 17 minutes, or until lightly browned.

While the lemon cups are baking, arrange the lemon leaves on 6 individual serving plates. Remove the lemon cups from the oven, arrange 2 on each plate, and top each lemon cup with 1 tablespoon Raspberry Sauce. Serve immediately. Makes 6 servings.

Each serving (2 lemon cups with sauce) contains about:
    108 calories
    54 mg sodium
    0 fat
    4 g protein
    21 g carbohydrate
    1 mg cholesterol

ORANGE SOUFFLE

  6 large, thick-skinned oranges
  ½ cup egg substitute (page 150), or 3 egg yolks
  ¼ cup fructose
  3 tablespoons cornstarch
  1 tablespoon orange-flavored liqueur
  ½ teaspoon cream of tartar
  3 egg whites, at room temperature
  Orange leaves with blossoms for garnish (optional)

With a sharp knife, cut 1 inch from the top of each orange. Then cut a thin round from the base so that the orange stands upright. With a grapefruit knife or a teaspoon, gently remove the pulp, taking care not to pierce the skins. Squeeze the pulp to obtain the juice, then strain the juice and set aside. Drain the shells upside down on paper toweling.

In a saucepan, beat together the egg substitute or yolks, fructose, and cornstarch. Stir in the reserved orange juice. Place over low heat, stirring constantly, until the mixture begins to boil and thicken. Remove from heat and let cool. (This mixture can be left to stand at this point until you wish to finish making the soufflés.)

About 30 minutes before serving, beat the egg whites at low speed until foamy. Add the cream of tartar and beat at high speed until stiff, glossy peaks form. Stir one-fourth of the egg white into the orange mixture to lighten it, then gently fold in the remaining whites. Fill the orange shells with the mixture. Place in a 9-by-13-inch shallow baking dish and bake in a 425°F oven for 10 to 12 minutes, or until lightly browned.

To serve, place each orange shell on an individual serving plate and garnish with orange leaves and blossoms. Serve immediately. Makes 6 servings.

Each serving contains about:
    103 calories
    46 mg sodium
    0 fat
    4 g protein
    18 g carbohydrate
    1 mg cholesterol

FROZEN HAZELNUT SOUFFLE

    ½ teaspoon low-calorie margarine (page 149)
    1¾ cups (1 can) peach nectar
    ¾ cup egg substitute (page 150), or 4 egg yolks, beaten
    2 cups Light Whipped Topping (page 145) or
        commercial low-calorie whipped topping
    ½ cup toasted blanched hazelnuts, finely chopped
    2 tablespoons peach-flavored brandy

Make a collar for a 1-quart soufflé dish by cutting a piece of foil long enough to encircle the dish with a 2-inch overlap and about 10 inches wide. Fold the foil in half lengthwise. Lightly grease one side of the foil and the inside of the soufflé dish with the margarine. Tape the foil firmly to the dish, greased side in, so that it stands 4 inches above the rim. Refrigerate until ready to fill.

Bring the peach nectar to a boil over medium-high heat and gently boil until it reduces to a syrup, about 5 minutes. Remove from the heat and let cool. Beat the egg substitute or yolks at high speed while slowly pouring in the peach nectar syrup. Continue to beat until the mixture is completely cool and stiff. Gently fold in all but ¼ cup of the whipped topping. Fold in the nuts and brandy. Spoon into the prepared soufflé dish and cover with the remaining whipped topping. Refrigerate for 6 hours or overnight. Remove the foil collar and serve immediately. Makes 6 servings.

Each ½ cup serving contains about:
185 calories
57 mg sodium
8 g fat
6 g protein
15 g carbohydrate
1 mg cholesterol

WINTER APRICOT SOUFFLE

½ cup dried apricots or commercial
    low-sugar apricot spread
3 tablespoons plus 1 teaspoon low-calorie
    margarine (page 149)
1 tablespoon cornstarch, dissolved in
    1 tablespoon water
¾ cup nonfat milk, scalded
2 tablespoons fresh lemon juice
¼ cup fructose
½ cup egg substitute (page 150), or
    3 egg yolks, beaten
4 egg whites, at room temperature
½ teaspoon cream of tartar

Place the apricots in a saucepan with enough water to cover generously. Bring to a boil, lower the heat, and simmer, uncovered, for 30 minutes. Remove from the heat, drain, purée in a food processor or blender, and set aside. (If you are using apricot spread, this step is unnecessary.) In a saucepan, melt 3 tablespoons of the margarine over medium heat. Add the cornstarch mixture and blend with a wire whisk. Cook, stirring with the whisk, until the mixture bubbles. Add the scalded milk and cook, stirring with the whisk, until the mixture thickens. Remove from the heat, add the lemon juice, fructose, and apricot purée or apricot spread and mix well. Let cool. Blend in the egg substitute or egg yolks.

In a small mixing bowl, beat the egg whites at low speed until foamy. Add the cream of tartar and beat at high speed until stiff, glossy peaks form. Stir one-fourth of the egg whites into the mixture to lighten it, then gently fold in the remaining whites. Grease a 1-quart soufflé dish or 6 individual soufflé dishes with the remaining margarine. Turn the soufflé mixture into the dish(es) and bake in a 375°F oven for 30 minutes, or until set and puffy. Remove from the oven and serve immediately. Makes 6 servings.

NOTE: When folding beaten egg whites into any mixture, use a rubber spatula. Gently scoop under the mixture and cut across the top surface, rotating the bowl after each fold. The object is to fold *just until* the egg whites are blended into the mixture and no white streaks remain. If you fold too long, the egg whites will deflate.

Each ½ cup serving contains about:
  98 calories
  52 mg sodium
  1 g fat
  4 g protein
  15 g carbohydrate
  1 mg cholesterol

HOT FRESH BLUEBERRY SOUFFLE

2 cups fresh blueberries, or
   1 (10-ounce) package unsweetened frozen
   blueberries, thawed
1 tablespoon fresh lemon juice
1 teaspoon freshly grated lemon zest
½ cup unsweetened cran-grape juice
2 teaspoons cornstarch, dissolved in 1 tablespoon water
¼ teaspoon almond extract
6 egg whites, at room temperature
1 teaspoon white vinegar
½ teaspoon low-calorie margarine (page 149)
Blueberry Sauce (following recipe)

Purée the blueberries, lemon juice, and lemon zest in a food processor or blender. In a saucepan, bring cran-grape juice to a boil. Stir in the cornstarch mixture, lower the heat, and cook, stirring constantly, until the grape juice is slightly thickened and syrupy. Combine the syrup and the blueberries and press the mixture through a fine sieve. Stir in the almond extract. Refrigerate or set in a bowl of ice water until cool.

Beat the egg whites at low speed until foamy. Add the vinegar and beat at high speed until stiff, glossy peaks form. Stir one-fourth of the egg whites into the blueberry mixture, then gently fold in the remaining whites. Grease a 1-quart soufflé dish or casserole with the margarine and turn the mixture into it. Bake in a 400°F oven for 25 minutes, or until set and puffy. Remove from the oven and serve immediately with 2 tablespoons warm Blueberry Sauce spooned over each serving. Makes 6 servings.

Blueberry Sauce

2 tablespoons fructose
1 tablespoon cornstarch
1½ teaspoons fresh lemon juice
¾ cup hot water
1 cup fresh or unsweetened frozen and
   thawed blueberries
1 tablespoon low-calorie margarine (page 149)
1 tablespoon brandy, Kirsch, or rum

While the soufflé is baking, make the sauce. Combine the fructose and cornstarch in a saucepan. Stir in the lemon juice until the cornstarch dissolves. Add the hot water and cook over medium heat, stirring constantly, until the mixture thickens. Add the blueberries, bring to a boil, and cook for 1 minute. Remove from the heat and stir in the margarine until it melts. Add the brandy and mix in well.

Each ½ cup serving with 2 tablespoons sauce contains about:
115 calories
51 mg sodium
0 fat
4 g protein
20 g carbohydrate
0 cholesterol

CHOCOLATE GRAND MARNIER SOUFFLE

1 tablespoon cornstarch
¾ cup nonfat milk
¼ cup semisweet chocolate or carob chips
3 tablespoons Grand Marnier
½ cup egg substitute (page 150), or 3 egg yolks, beaten
4 egg whites, at room temperature
½ teaspoon cream of tartar
½ teaspoon low-calorie margarine (page 149)

In a saucepan, combine the cornstarch and milk and stir until the cornstarch dissolves. Bring to a boil, lower the heat, and cook, stirring constantly, until thickened. Add the chocolate and Grand Marnier, remove from the heat, and stir until the chocolate melts. Cool slightly and mix in the egg substitute or egg yolks, 1 tablespoon at a time or 1 yolk at a time. Set aside.

Beat the egg whites at low speed until foamy. Add the cream of tartar and beat at high speed until stiff, glossy peaks form. Stir one-fourth of the egg whites into the cooled chocolate mixture to lighten it, then gently fold in the remaining whites. Grease a 1-quart soufflé dish or 6 individual soufflé dishes with the margarine and turn the mixture into the dish(es). Bake in a 350°F oven for 15 minutes for individual soufflés and 35 to 40 minutes for a large soufflé, or until set and puffy. Remove from the oven and serve immediately. Makes 6 servings.

Each ½ cup serving contains about:
106 calories
28 mg sodium
3 g fat
5 g protein
9 g carbohydrate
1 mg cholesterol

MOCHA SOUFFLE

1 tablespoon cornstarch
1 tablespoon fructose
½ cup nonfat milk
¼ cup evaporated nonfat milk
⅓ cup semisweet chocolate or carob chips
3 tablespoons coffee-flavored liqueur
1 teaspoon pure vanilla extract
3 egg whites, at room temperature
¼ teaspoon cream of tartar
½ teaspoon low-calorie margarine (page 149)

In a saucepan, combine the cornstarch, fructose, and milks and stir until the cornstarch dissolves. Bring to a boil, lower the heat, and cook, stirring constantly, until thickened. Add the chocolate chips, liqueur, and vanilla extract. Remove from the heat and stir until the chocolate melts. Let cool.

Beat the egg whites at low speed until foamy. Add the cream of tartar and beat at high speed until stiff, glossy peaks form. Stir one-fourth of the whites into the cooled chocolate mixture to lighten it, then gently fold in the remaining whites. Grease a 1-quart soufflé dish or 6 individual soufflé dishes with the margarine. Turn the mixture into the dish(es) and bake in a 350°F oven for 10 to 15 minutes for individual soufflés and 40 minutes for a large soufflé, or until set and puffy. Remove from the oven and serve immediately. Makes 6 servings.

Each ½ cup serving contains about:
   79 calories
   48 mg sodium
   3 g fat
   3 g protein
   8 g carbohydrate
   1 mg cholesterol

VERY SIMPLE STRAWBERRY SOUFFLE

**16 ounces (2 jars) commercial low-sugar strawberry
   jelly spread
5 egg whites, at room temperature
¼ teaspoon cream of tartar
½ teaspoon low-calorie margarine (page 149)**

Beat the strawberry jelly with a wire whisk or spoon until it is free of
lumps. Beat the egg whites at low speed until foamy. Add the cream
of tartar and beat at high speed until stiff, glossy peaks form. Stir
one-fourth of the egg whites into the jelly mixture to lighten it, then
gently fold in the remaining whites. Grease a 1½-quart soufflé dish
with the margarine and turn the mixture into it. Bake in a 325°F
oven for 15 minutes, or until the top is lightly browned. Remove
from the oven and serve immediately. Makes 6 servings.
   NOTE: Any flavor low-sugar jelly, such as blueberry, may be used.

Each ½ cup serving contains about:
   37 calories
   42 mg sodium
   0 fat
   3 g protein
   5 g carbohydrate
   0 cholesterol

Crêpes & Mousses

Crêpes are a good low-calorie, low-cholesterol dessert for informal parties. These simple pancakes of flour, nonfat milk, and eggs or egg substitute offer almost limitless possibilities. Prepare a quantity of crêpes, arrange them on a buffet table with a selection of fillings and toppings, and let guests assemble their own.

Crêpes are ideal do-ahead fare. Stack the freshly cooked crêpes between sheets of waxed paper or aluminum foil and let cool. Seal tightly in plastic bags and refrigerate for up to four days or wrap the filled plastic bags with freezer paper and freeze several months. Bring to room temperature before filling to avoid tearing.

LIGHT CREPES

2¼ cups unbleached flour
1¼ cups nonfat milk
½ cup water
½ cup unsweetened orange juice
¼ cup plus 2 tablespoons egg substitute (page 150), or
    2 eggs, beaten
1 tablespoon vegetable oil
2 teaspoons low-calorie margarine (page 149)

In a food processor or blender, combine the flour, milk, water, orange juice, egg substitute or eggs, and oil. Beat until well blended and smooth. Chill the batter for 30 minutes.

Lightly grease a 6-inch nonstick skillet or crêpe pan with a little of the margarine and place over medium heat until pan is hot. Remove from the heat and spoon in about 2 tablespoons of the batter. Lift and tilt the skillet to spread the batter evenly over the pan bottom. Return the pan to medium heat and cook the crêpe until lightly browned on the underside. Turn crêpe out onto paper toweling (it will slide easily from pan when done). Repeat until all the crêpes are cooked, greasing the skillet as necessary with the remaining margarine. Makes about 30 crêpes.

VARIATION: Proceed as directed for Light Crêpes, substituting whole-wheat flour for the unbleached flour and increasing the water to 3/4 cup.

Each crêpe contains about:
40 calories
8 mg sodium
1 g fat
1 g protein
7 g carbohydrate
0 cholesterol

CHOCOLATE MOUSSE–FILLED CREPES

6 Light Crêpes (page 42)
¾ cup Chocolate Mousse (page 58)
½ cup Light Whipped Topping (page 145) or
    commercial low-calorie whipped topping
1 tablespoon chopped toasted almonds

Spoon 2 tablespoons of mousse on each crêpe, roll up, and arrange on a serving plate. Top each crêpe with a dollop of whipped topping and ½ teaspoon almonds. Serve at once. Makes 6 servings.

Each serving contains about:
99 calories
45 mg sodium
5 g fat
4 g protein
12 g carbohydrate
0 cholesterol

BANANA CREAM CREPES

6 Light Crêpes (page 42)
1 cup low-fat vanilla yogurt, Light Whipped Topping
    (page 145), or commercial low-calorie whipped
    topping
1 teaspoon pure vanilla extract, or
    1½ tablespoons banana liqueur
    (crème de banane)
1½ medium bananas, thinly sliced
2 tablespoons Chocolate Sauce (page 142, optional)

Combine the yogurt and vanilla extract. Fold in the sliced bananas. Spoon about 2 tablespoons of the mixture on each crêpe, roll up, and arrange on a serving dish. Pour chocolate sauce over the top, if desired. Makes 6 servings.

Each serving contains about:
    89 calories
    28 mg sodium
    1 g fat
    3 g protein
    16 g carbohydrate
    4 mg cholesterol

VARIATIONS

Apple Crêpes: Fill each crêpe with 2 tablespoons Apple Purée Glaze (page 65). Top with a dollop of low-fat apple yogurt.

Peach Crêpes: Fill each crêpe with 2 tablespoons chopped fresh peaches. Top with a dollop of low-fat peach yogurt.

Raspberry or Strawberry Crêpes: Fill each crêpe with 2 tablespoons fresh raspberries or sliced fresh strawberries. Top with a dollop of low-fat raspberry or strawberry yogurt.

NORMANDY PANCAKES

16 Light Crêpes (page 42)
1 tablespoon low-calorie margarine (page 149)
3 dessert apples (Pippin, Rome Beauty, or apple
     of choice), peeled and thinly sliced
1 cup unsweetened apple juice
1 tablespoon cornstarch, dissolved in
     1 tablespoon water
1½ teaspoons maple extract
1 tablespoon fructose
⅓ cup low-fat apple yogurt
⅓ cup Calvados, or ⅓ cup rum, plus
     1 tablespoon unsweetened apple juice

Melt the margarine in a nonstick skillet, add the apples and apple juice, and mix gently. Cover and cook over low heat until apples are soft, about 10 minutes. Mix together the cornstarch mixture, maple extract, and fructose. Stir into the apple mixture and cook, stirring, until thickened. Remove from the heat and stir in the yogurt.

Spread 2 tablespoons of the apple mixture on each crêpe and roll up. Arrange the crêpes in an ovenproof dish and heat for 5 minutes in a moderately hot (375°F) oven. Remove from the oven, sprinkle with the Calvados, and carefully ignite. When the flame dies out, serve immediately. Makes 8 servings.

Each serving (2 pancakes) contains about:
    168 calories
    20 mg sodium
    2 g fat
    2 g protein
    29 g carbohydrate
    1 mg cholesterol

BLUEBERRY CHEESE BLINTZES

Wonderful for a Sunday brunch.

   20 Light Crêpes (page 42)
   1½ cups ricotta cheese (made from partially skimmed
       milk) or low-fat cottage cheese
   2 tablespoons fructose
   ½ teaspoon ground cinnamon
   1 tablespoon Low-Calorie Margarine (page 149)
   1½ cups fresh or unsweetened frozen and thawed
       blueberries, dried thoroughly
   ¾ cup low-fat vanilla or blueberry yogurt

Mix together the ricotta cheese, fructose, and cinnamon. Place a
spoonful of filling on each crêpe, fold in ends, and roll up. Melt the
margarine in a nonstick saucepan and sauté blintzes until golden.
Place the blintzes on a hot serving platter. Top each blintz with some
of the blueberries and about 1 tablespoon of the yogurt. Serve hot.
Makes 10 servings.

   Each serving (2 blintzes) contains about:
      169 calories
      31 mg sodium
      4 g fat
      8 g protein
      23 g carbohydrate
      14 mg cholesterol

MOCHA-FILLED CREPES WITH
MAPLE-WALNUT CREAM

   6 Light Crêpes (page 42)
   6 tablespoons Chocolate or Carob Sauce
       (page 142, optional)
   ¾ cup Coffee Bean Ice Cream (page 126), softened
       slightly, or low-fat coffee yogurt
   6 tablespoons Maple-Walnut Cream (page 140)

Spoon 2 tablespoons of the ice cream on each crêpe, roll up, and place on 6 individual serving plates. Top each crêpe with 1 tablespoon each of Maple-Walnut Cream and Chocolate Sauce, if desired. Makes 6 servings.

, Each serving, with cream and sauce, contains approximately:
    131 calories
    71 mg sodium
    3 g fat
    5 g protein
    20 g carbohydrate
    3 mg cholesterol

VARIATIONS

Apple Ice Cream Crêpes: Fill each crêpe with 2 tablespoons Apple Ice Cream (page 123). Top with 1 tablespoon Apricot Sauce (page 141).

Each crêpe contains about:
    61 calories
    20 mg sodium
    1 g fat
    1 g protein
    12 g carbohydrate
    0 cholesterol

Rich Chocolate Ice Cream Crêpes: Fill each crêpe with 2 tablespoons Rich Carob or Chocolate Ice Cream (page 122). Top with 1 tablespoon Maple-Walnut Cream (page 140).

Each crêpe contains about:
    127 calories
    34 mg sodium
    4 g fat
    3 g protein
    21 g carbohydrate
    1 mg cholesterol

CREPES SUZETTE

12 Light Crêpes (page 42)
¼ cup low-calorie margarine (page 149)
2 tablespoons fructose
Grated zest of 1 orange
½ cup unsweetened orange juice
½ teaspoon fresh lemon juice
2 tablespoons orange-flavored liqueur
1 tablespoon brandy or cognac

In a large nonstick skillet, mix together the margarine and fructose. Mix in the orange zest. Gradually add the orange juice, lemon juice, and liqueur and blend well. Set the sauce aside until serving time.

To serve, heat the sauce until bubbly. Add the crêpes, one at a time, turning each to coat with the sauce. After coating with the sauce, fold each crêpe in half, then in half again so it is folded into quarters. Remove the crêpe to a warmed serving platter and repeat until all the crêpes have been folded.

In a small saucepan, heat the brandy and pour it over the crêpes. Ignite the brandy and spoon it over the crêpes until the flame dies. Transfer 2 crêpes to each of 6 warmed individual plates and unfold once so that they are only folded in half. Spoon some of the sauce over each serving. Makes 6 servings.

Each serving contains about:
136 calories
14 mg sodium
2 g fat
2 g protein
20 g carbohydrate
0 cholesterol

APRICOT CREPES FLAMBE

12 Light Crêpes (page 42)
2 tablespoons low-calorie unsalted margarine (page 149)
¼ cup commercial low-sugar apricot spread
1 tablespoon plus 2 teaspoons dark rum
2 tablespoons orange-flavored liqueur

In a small mixing bowl, blend together the margarine, apricot spread, and 2 teaspoons of the rum. Spread 2 teaspoons of the mixture on the lower third of each crêpe. Roll up the crêpes and arrange in an ovenproof dish (crêpes may be refrigerated at this point).

About 10 minutes before serving time, heat the crêpes in a 375°F oven for 10 minutes, or until they are heated through. In a small saucepan, warm together the liqueur and remaining rum. Bring the crêpes to the table, pour warmed spirits over, and carefully ignite. Spoon the sauce over the crêpes until the flame dies out. Transfer 2 crêpes to each of 6 individual warmed serving plates and spoon some of the sauce over each. Makes 6 servings.

NOTE: Low-sugar strawberry spread may be substituted for the apricot spread and Kirsch may be substituted for the rum.

Each serving (2 crêpes) contains about:
    124 calories
    17 mg sodium
    1 g fat
    2 g protein
    16 g carbohydrate
    0 cholesterol

VANILLA-WHITE CHOCOLATE MOUSSE

1 vanilla bean
1 tablespoon fructose
4 ounces (4 squares) white chocolate, coarsely chopped
½ cup plus 1 tablespoon egg substitute (page 150), or
    3 egg yolks
3 egg whites, at room temperature
¼ teaspoon cream of tartar

¼ cup semisweet chocolate or carob chips
3 tablespoons nonfat milk, hot
6 tablespoons pistachio nuts, ground (optional)

At least 2 days ahead, combine the vanilla bean and fructose in a food processor or blender and mix until finely ground. Pass through a fine sieve, reserving large pieces of vanilla for another use. Transfer vanilla-fructose mixture to an airtight container. Let stand until ready to use, preferably several days or longer.

Melt the white chocolate in a small bowl set over hot (not boiling) water, stirring constantly until smooth. Let cool slightly. In a medium bowl, combine the egg substitute or yolks with vanilla-fructose mixture. Beat until well blended. Beat the egg whites at low speed until foamy. Add the cream of tartar and beat at high speed until stiff, glossy peaks form. Stir one-fourth of the egg whites into the chocolate mixture to lighten it, then gently fold in the remaining whites. Spoon ½ cup of the mixture into each of 6 individual goblets. Cover and refrigerate until set, about 2 hours or, preferably, overnight.

About 5 minutes before serving, combine the semisweet chocolate and hot milk in a food processor or blender and blend until smooth. Spoon 1 tablespoon over each serving and sprinkle ground pistachios in the center. Makes 6 servings.

NOTE: One teaspoon pure vanilla extract may be substituted for the vanilla bean. Add the extract with the fructose to the egg substitute.

Each ½ cup serving contains about:
178 calories
52 mg sodium
13 g fat
6 g protein
13 g carbohydrate
1 mg cholesterol

APPLE MOUSSE

    4 medium Pippin apples, peeled and sliced
    2 tablespoons commercial low-sugar apricot spread
    1 tablespoon water
    ¼ teaspoon freshly grated lemon zest
    ½ teaspoon ground cinnamon
    Pinch of ground nutmeg
1½ cups nonfat milk
    1 envelope (1 tablespoon) unflavored gelatin
    6 tablespoons egg substitute (page 150), or
        4 egg yolks, beaten
    ¼ cup fructose
    1 teaspoon pure vanilla extract
1½ cups Light Whipped Topping (page 145) or
        commercial low-calorie whipped topping
    ½ cup Apricot Sauce (page 141, optional)

In a large saucepan, combine the apples, apricot spread, water, and lemon zest. Cover and cook over very low heat until apples are very soft, stirring frequently to prevent scorching. Transfer mixture to a food processor or blender and purée. Add the cinnamon and nutmeg. Chill.

Sprinkle the gelatin over 2 tablespoons of the milk. In a saucepan, combine the egg substitute or yolks and fructose and whisk until well blended and smooth. Add the remaining milk and cook over low heat, stirring frequently, until mixture comes to a simmer, about 10 minutes. Add the softened gelatin and vanilla extract and whisk until gelatin dissolves, about 2 minutes. Transfer the mixture to a large bowl and chill until it just begins to set. Whisk until smooth, add the apple purée, and whisk gently to blend. Taste and add more nutmeg and cinnamon, if desired. Fold the whipped topping into the apple mixture. Pour into a lightly greased 4-cup mold and chill.

Just before serving, invert onto a serving platter. (To facilitate unmolding, wrap a hot damp towel around the bottom of the mold and shake the mold to loosen the mousse.) Spoon the Apricot Sauce around the mousse, if desired. Makes 8 servings.

CALORIE-, FAT-, AND CHOLESTEROL-SAVING TIP: In recipes calling for milk, use nonfat milk in place of whole milk to reduce calories, fat, and cholesterol.

Each ½ cup serving, with sauce, contains about:
    114 calories
    51 mg sodium
    2 g fat
    5 g protein
    21 g carbohydrate
    1 mg cholesterol

POTS DE CREME DE CACAO

If you think chocolate is the first thing to cut from a calorie-shy diet, consider this light, low-calorie dessert. It is made without cream, so you can enjoy the flavor of traditional chocolate mousse, and save more than 200 calories.

    3 tablespoons crème de cacao liqueur
    1½ teaspoons unflavored gelatin
    ¾ cup hot brewed decaffeinated coffee
    1 cup Rich Carob or Chocolate Ice Cream (page 122)

Combine the liqueur and gelatin in a food processor or blender container, wait 1 minute, then add the hot coffee. Cover and blend until gelatin dissolves. Add the ice cream, cover, and blend until smooth. Pour into 4 custard cups and chill until set, about 2 hours. Makes 4 servings.

NOTE: Three tablespoons nonfat milk or melted chocolate ice cream may be substituted for liqueur.

Each ½ cup serving contains about:
    52 calories
    11 mg sodium
    0 fat
    2 g protein
    7 g carbohydrate
    0 cholesterol

FROZEN APRICOT MOUSSE

½ cup firmly packed dried apricots
½ cup water
¼ cup fructose
1 teaspoon pure vanilla extract
1 teaspoon fresh lemon juice
1 cup apricot nectar
¾ cup egg substitute (page 150), or
    4 egg yolks, beaten
3 egg whites, at room temperature
1 cup Light Whipped Topping (page 145) or
    commercial low-calorie whipped topping
6 tablespoons Apricot Sauce (page 141, optional)

In a saucepan, bring the apricots and water to a boil. Lower the heat, cover, and simmer for 10 minutes. Add 2 tablespoons of the fructose and stir until it dissolves. Remove the saucepan from the heat and add the vanilla extract. Transfer the mixture to a food processor or blender and blend until puréed. Add the lemon juice and enough apricot nectar for the mixture to measure 2 cups. Blend until smooth. Gradually add the egg substitute or yolks to the apricot mixture and blend until smooth with a wire whisk. Transfer the mixture to the top pan of a double boiler placed over simmering water. Cook over low heat, stirring constantly, until very thick, about 15 minutes. Remove the top of the double boiler from the heat and set in a bowl of ice. Stir until the mixture cools.

Beat the egg whites at medium speed until soft peaks form. Gradually adding the remaining fructose, beat at high speed until stiff, glossy peaks form. Stir one-fourth of the egg whites into the apricot mixture to lighten it, then fold in the remaining whites. Fold the whipped topping into the apricot mixture. Pour ¾ cup of the mixture into each of 8 dessert glasses. Cover and freeze overnight.

Just before serving, top each serving with some of the Apricot Sauce, if desired. Makes 8 servings.

Each ¾ cup serving with sauce contains about:
    98 calories
    54 mg sodium
    1 g fat
    4 g protein
    16 g carbohydrate
    1 mg cholesterol

PEACH MOUSSE

2 large plums
4 medium fresh peaches, or
    8 unsweetened frozen and thawed or
    water-packed canned peach halves
1 tablespoon fresh lemon juice
½ cup unsweetened orange juice
2 envelopes (2 tablespoons) unflavored gelatin
¼ cup cold water
¼ cup fructose
2 tablespoons cognac (optional)
¼ teaspoon almond extract
3 egg whites, at room temperature
1 cup Light Whipped Topping (page 145) or
    commercial low-calorie whipped topping

Peel, pit, and cut up the plums and 3 of the peaches (or 6 halves). Place in the container of a food processor or blender with the lemon juice and ¼ cup of the orange juice, and blend just until the fruit is evenly chopped. Do not purée it.

In a saucepan, soften the gelatin in the cold water. Boil the remaining ¼ cup of orange juice, add it to the gelatin, and place over low heat, stirring, until the gelatin dissolves.

In a bowl, combine the gelatin mixture and the fruit mixture. Stir in the fructose, cognac, and almond extract. Cover and chill until very thick and almost set. Stir.

In a small bowl, beat the egg whites at high speed until stiff, glossy peaks form. Stir one-fourth of the egg whites into the fruit mixture to lighten it, then gently fold in the remaining whites. Fold the whipped topping into the egg white mixture. Pour 3/4 cup into each of 8 long-stemmed parfait glasses. Cover and refrigerate for several hours, or until set.

To serve, peel and slice the remaining peach or slice the halves and decorate each serving with a peach slice. Makes 8 servings.

NOTE: If plums are not available, use 2 additional peaches. For directions on peeling peaches, see page 2.

Each ¾ cup serving contains about:
    80 calories
    30 mg sodium
    1 g fat

Pecan Ice Cream Log

Poached Pears in Chocolate Sauce

4 g protein
16 g carbohydrate
0 cholesterol

MELON MOUSSE

1 medium cantaloupe or other ripe sweet melon,
    peeled, seeded and coarsely chopped
Juice of ½ lemon
2 teaspoons chopped fresh mint
½ teaspoon unflavored gelatin
1 cup Light Whipped Topping (page 145) or
    commercial low-calorie whipped topping
3 small cantaloupes or other ripe sweet melons,
    halved and seeded
Mint sprigs for garnish

Purée the chopped melon in a food processor or blender until smooth, stopping occasionally to scrape down sides of container. You should have 2 cups purée. Transfer the purée to a small bowl and add the lemon juice and chopped mint. Marinate at room temperature several hours. Press through a fine sieve and transfer to a small saucepan. Sprinkle with gelatin and let stand several minutes to soften. Place over low heat and stir until gelatin dissolves. Refrigerate until cooled and just slightly thickened, about 15 minutes.

Stir one-fourth of the whipped topping into the melon purée to lighten it, then gently fold in the remaining topping. Cover and refrigerate for several hours or overnight, folding occasionally.

To serve, mound mousse in melon halves and garnish with a sprig of mint. Makes 6 servings.

Each serving contains about:
    58 calories
    30 mg sodium
    1 g fat
    2 g protein
    12 g carbohydrate
    0 cholesterol

RASPBERRY MOUSSE

1 cup fresh raspberries, or 1 (10-ounce) package
    unsweetened frozen raspberries, thawed
1 cup Light Whipped Topping (page 145) or
    commercial low-calorie whipped topping
3 egg whites, at room temperature
¼ cup fructose
6 tablespoons Raspberry Sauce (page 141) for
    garnish (optional)
12 fresh raspberries for garnish
Fresh mint leaves for garnish

Purée 1 cup of raspberries in a food processor or blender. Fold the purée into the whipped topping. Beat the egg whites at medium speed until soft peaks form. Gradually adding the fructose, beat at high speed until stiff, glossy peaks form. Stir one-fourth of the egg whites into the raspberry mixture to lighten it, then gently fold in the remaining whites. Turn the mixture into a plastic container, cover, and freeze until firm.

To serve, spoon ½ cup of the raspberry mixture into each of 8 dessert glasses and, if desired, garnish each serving with 1 table-spoon Raspberry Sauce, 2 whole raspberries and a mint leaf. Makes 8 servings.

Each ½ cup serving with sauce contains about:
    90 calories
    29 mg sodium
    1 g fat
    2 g protein
    20 g carbohydrate
    0 cholesterol

CHOCOLATE MOUSSETTES

15 Nabisco Famous Chocolate Wafers, finely crushed
1¼ cups semisweet chocolate or carob chips
¼ cup cold brewed decaffeinated coffee (optional)
1½ cups egg substitute (page 150), or 8 egg yolks
1 teaspoon pure vanilla extract
4 egg whites, at room temperature
1 teaspoon white vinegar
1½ cups Light Whipped Topping (page 145) or
    commercial low-calorie whipped topping

Line 30 muffin-tin wells with foil-lined paper cups and put 1 tablespoon crushed wafer into each one. With your fingertips, press the crumbs evenly over the bottom of each cup. Set aside.

Melt the chocolate in the top pan of a double boiler placed over simmering water and blend in coffee, if desired. Add the egg substitute, a little at a time, or the egg yolks, one at a time, blending well after each addition. Stir in the vanilla extract, remove from the heat, and let cool. Beat the egg whites at low speed until foamy. Add the vinegar and beat at high speed until stiff, glossy peaks form. Stir one-fourth of the egg whites into the chocolate mixture to lighten it, then gently fold in the remaining whites. Spoon into the prepared paper cups, cover, and freeze until firm.

To serve, remove from muffin tins and garnish each of the cups with 1 tablespoon whipped topping. Makes 30 moussettes.

CALORIE- AND FAT-SAVING TIP: Use sweetened cocoa powder instead of chocolate chips to reduce calories and saturated fat. For each 2 tablespoons of chocolate, use 3 tablespoons cocoa powder plus 1 tablespoon low-calorie margarine (page 149). Place over simmering water in a double boiler and cook, stirring constantly, until smooth.

Each moussette contains about:
118 calories
38 mg sodium
3 g fat
2 g protein
7 g carbohydrate
0 cholesterol

CHOCOLATE MOUSSE

½ cup nonfat milk, hot
¾ cup semisweet chocolate or carob chips
½ cup plus 1 tablespoon egg substitute (page 150), or
    3 egg yolks
1 teaspoon pure vanilla extract
2 cups Light Whipped Topping (page 145) or
    commercial low-calorie whipped topping

In a food processor or blender, combine the hot milk and chocolate. Process until the chocolate has completely melted and the mixture is blended. Add the egg substitute, ¼ cup at a time, or the egg yolks, 1 yolk at a time, and blend for 1 or 2 seconds after each addition. Add the vanilla extract and blend again. Fold the chocolate mixture into the whipped topping. Pour into a 1-quart container, cover, and freeze for 2 hours or longer.

Twenty-five minutes before serving time, remove the container from the freezer and refrigerate it. To serve, spoon the mousse into 8 dessert glasses. Makes 8 servings.

CALORIE-, CHOLESTEROL-, SALT-, AND FAT-SAVING TIP: Egg substitute (page 150) can be used in any recipe calling for eggs to lower calories, cholesterol, and saturated fat. If using commercial egg substitute, compare labels for calorie and sodium content. Use 3 tablespoons (1½ ounces) egg substitute for each egg.

Each ½ cup serving contains about:
    132 calories
    46 mg sodium
    7 g fat
    4 g protein
    13 g carbohydrate
    1 mg cholesterol

Baked Desserts

TART PASTRY

Good pastry crusts are characteristically difficult to make and high in calories and fat. However, a crispy, light, delicious crust can be made with baking powder and low-calorie margarine.

> ¾ cup unbleached flour
> ½ teaspoon low-sodium baking powder (page 164) or regular baking powder
> 1 tablespoon fructose
> 6 tablespoons low-calorie margarine (page 149)
> 1 egg white, lightly beaten

Combine the flour, baking powder, and fructose in a small mixing bowl. Add the margarine to the flour mixture and stir with a fork until evenly distributed and mixture is crumbly. Pat into a ball, wrap, and chill for 1 hour.

Place the dough between 2 sheets of waxed paper and roll out one 10-inch circle or eight 3-inch circles. Invert the large circle into a 9-inch flan pan with a removable bottom and the small ones into 2½-inch tart tins or muffin cups. Prick the pastry in several places with a fork to allow steam to escape during baking. Bake in a 400°F oven for 15 minutes, or until golden brown. Remove from the oven and brush with the egg white. Let cool before adding filling. Makes one 9-inch tart shell or eight 2½-inch tart shells.

NOTE: If on an extremely low-sodium diet, purchase low-sodium baking powder or have your druggist make it for you (page 164).

CALORIE-SAVING TIP: Rolling out pastry on a floured surface adds hidden calories to your dessert. To avoid those calories, place the dough between 2 sheets of waxed paper and roll it out to necessary size and shape. Remove the top sheet and invert pastry into tart pan. Peel off remaining paper and ease the pastry into the pan.

Each serving (one 2½-inch tart shell or one-eighth of a 9-inch tart shell) contains about:
- 77 calories
- 27 mg sodium
- 1 g fat
- 1 g protein
- 9 g carbohydrate
- 0 cholesterol

TARTE A L'ORANGE

½ cup ricotta cheese (made with partially skimmed
  milk) or low-fat cottage cheese
½ cup low-fat or vanilla yogurt
5 small thin-skinned oranges, thinly sliced
1 prebaked 9-inch tart pastry shell (page 60),
  with 1 teaspoon fresh finely grated orange zest and
  ¼ teaspoon almond extract added to the dough
⅓ cup commercial low-sugar apricot spread
1½ tablespoons orange-flavored liqueur or
  unsweetened orange juice

Combine the ricotta cheese and yogurt and mix until smooth (overmixing will cause the mixture to become too liquid). Evenly spread the cheese-yogurt mixture into the cooled tart shell. Arrange the orange slices in an attractive pinwheel pattern over the cheese-yogurt mixture.

In a saucepan, bring the apricot spread to a boil. Press through a fine sieve. Combine the apricot spread and the liqueur in a saucepan and bring the mixture to a simmer. Brush evenly and thinly over the orange slices. Makes 8 servings.

Each serving contains about:
  126 calories
  34 mg sodium
  3 g fat
  3 g protein
  14 g carbohydrate
  6 mg cholesterol

COUNTRY PEAR TART

Pastry dough for one 9-inch tart pastry shell (page 60)
1 tablespoon low-calorie unsalted margarine (page 149)
¾ cup pear nectar
2 teaspoons cornstarch, dissolved in 1 teaspoon water
½ teaspoon maple extract
4 firm, ripe fresh pears, peeled and quartered, or
    8 water-packed canned pear halves,
    drained and halved
½ teaspoon ground cinnamon
½ cup Light Whipped Topping (page 145) or
    commercial low-calorie whipped topping (optional)

Place chilled pastry dough between sheets of waxed paper and roll dough out to ⅛ inch thickness. Using an inverted 9-inch metal cake pan as a guide, cut out a circle to form a crust. Refrigerate until ready to use.

Melt the margarine in a 9-inch cake pan over low heat. Mix in the pear nectar, cornstarch mixture and maple extract. Stir over medium heat until mixture thickens slightly. Arrange pears evenly in the pan, rounded side down. Sprinkle with the cinnamon. Carefully lay the prepared crust over the pears and prick in several places to allow steam to escape. Bake in a 375°F oven for 35 to 45 minutes, or until the crust is evenly browned. Remove from the oven and cool 5 minutes. Carefully invert tart onto a serving platter. Serve at room temperature with a dollop of whipped topping, if desired. Makes 8 servings.

Each serving contains about:
  142 calories
  28 mg sodium

2 g fat
1 g protein
24 g carbohydrate
0 cholesterol

GLAZED SUMMER- OR
WINTER-FRUIT TARTLETS

¼ cup strawberry nectar, if using red fruits
¼ cup apricot nectar, if using light-colored fruits
1½ teaspoons cornstarch
1 cup Light Whipped Topping (page 145), Special
    Cream (page 148), Custard Sauce (page 147), or
    commercial low-calorie whipped topping
8 prebaked 2½-inch tart pastry shells (page 60)
2 cups fresh strawberries, raspberries, blueberries, or
    boysenberries, left whole, halved, or sliced,
    or 4 ripe kiwis, peeled and halved or sliced,
    or 4 ripe fresh freestone peaches, nectarines,
    apples, apricots, or pears, peeled, pitted or cored, and
    halved or sliced

In a saucepan, combine the strawberry or apricot nectar, depending on the color of fruit to be used, with the cornstarch. Stir until the cornstarch dissolves. Cook over medium heat, stirring constantly, until the mixture thickens and becomes glossy. Remove from the heat and cool slightly. Spoon the whipped topping into the cooled shells, filling them halfway. Arrange the fruit, rounded side up, attractively over the filling. Brush the fruit with the strawberry or apricot glaze. Refrigerate until ready to serve. Makes 8 servings.

NOTE: Substitute ¼ cup commercial low-sugar strawberry or apricot spread for the strawberry or apricot nectar. If using low-sugar spread, omit the cornstarch and melt the spread with 1 tablespoon water in a small saucepan. Press through a fine sieve and brush the melted spread over the fruit.

Substitute unsweetened frozen and thawed or water-packed canned and drained fruits for the fresh fruits.

CALORIE-SAVING TIP: Fruits (dried, fresh, or unsweetened canned or frozen) have natural sweetness. Use unsweetened fruit and fruit juices to sweeten sauces.

Each tart contains about:
   133 calories
   38 mg sodium
   2 g fat
   2 g protein
   24 g carbohydrate
   0 cholesterol

FRESH APPLE TART

Apple Purée Glaze (following recipe)
2 tablespoons unsweetened frozen apple juice
   concentrate, thawed
3 medium Pippin apples, peeled and sliced paper thin
One 9-inch tart pastry shell, baked just until pastry
   begins to color, about 5 minutes (page 60)
Ground cinnamon
1 tablespoon fresh lemon or lime juice
1 cup Special Cream (page 148) or
   low-fat flavored yogurt of choice (optional)

Prepare the Apple Purée Glaze and set aside. Heat 1 tablespoon of the apple juice concentrate in a large nonstick skillet over medium-low heat. Add half of the apple slices and sauté just until softened. Remove with a slotted spoon. Repeat with the remaining tablespoon of apple juice concentrate and apple slices. Arrange the apple slices over the cooled tart shell and sprinkle with cinnamon and lemon juice. Bake in a 425°F oven until pastry is golden and apples are cooked but not mushy, about 20 to 25 minutes. Remove from the oven and heat the glaze, stirring constantly. Spread the glaze over the apples. Serve hot or cold, with a dollop of Special Cream on each serving, if desired. Makes 8 servings.

Each serving without Special Cream contains about:
   131 calories
   28 mg sodium
   2 g fat
   1 g protein
   23 g carbohydrate
   0 cholesterol

Apple Purée Glaze

1½ cups peeled and coarsely chopped Red or Golden
    Delicious apples (1½ medium apples)
½ cup unsweetened frozen apple juice
    concentrate, thawed

Combine the chopped apples and apple juice concentrate in a sauce-pan and simmer, stirring frequently, until thick. Transfer to a food processor or blender and purée until smooth. Return to the saucepan and set aside.

STRAWBERRY TART

This luscious tart tastes as if it is loaded with calories. But because the pastry is made with a small amount of low-calorie margarine rather than butter or oil and the filling is made with yogurt rather than cream, it's a calorie bargain. A traditional fruit pie would have about 350 calories a slice.

½ cup ricotta cheese (made with partially skimmed
    milk) or low-fat cottage cheese
½ cup low-fat strawberry yogurt
1 prebaked 9-inch tart pastry shell (page 60)
4 cups fresh strawberries, hulled
⅓ cup commercial low-sugar strawberry spread
1 tablespoon water

Combine the ricotta cheese and low-fat yogurt and mix until smooth (overmixing will cause the mixture to be too liquid). To assemble, place the cooled tart shell on a serving platter. Spread the cheese-yogurt mixture ⅛ inch thick over the entire inside surface of the shell. Place the strawberries, stem ends down, in a concentric circle to cover the top. Melt the strawberry spread and water over low heat. Press through a fine sieve and brush over the strawberries and outer edge of the crust to glaze completely. Refrigerate the tart until ready to serve. Makes 8 servings.

VARIATION: 6 kiwis, peeled and thinly sliced, may be substituted for the strawberries.

CALORIE-, FAT-, AND CHOLESTEROL-SAVING TIP: Use

low-fat or nonfat dairy products to reduce calories, fat, and cholesterol.

Each serving contains about:
135 calories
39 mg sodium
3 g fat
4 g protein
18 g carbohydrate
5 mg cholesterol

BRANDIED PEACH TART

This is an easy-to-prepare, nutritious, rich, elegant dessert.

¾ **cup low-fat peach yogurt**
¼ **cup low-fat plain yogurt**
1 **prebaked 9-inch tart pastry shell (page 60)**
5 **ripe fresh freestone peaches, or 1 (1-pound, 13-ounce)**
    can water-packed peach halves, drained
1 **tablespoon apricot-flavored brandy**
¼ **cup commercial low-sugar apricot spread**

Mix together the peach and plain yogurts (overmixing will cause the mixture to be too liquid). Spread a ½-inch-thick layer of the yogurt mixture in the cooled tart shell. Immerse the fresh peaches in a bowl of boiling water for 30 seconds, remove, peel, halve, and pit. Arrange a layer of peaches, rounded sides up, over the yogurt. Combine the brandy and apricot spread in a small saucepan and melt over low heat. Press it through a fine sieve and brush over the peaches. Chill before serving. Makes 8 servings.

Each serving contains about:
135 calories
42 mg sodium
2 g fat
3 g protein
20 g carbohydrate
3 mg cholesterol

SAVARIN WITH BLUEBERRIES

2 cups unbleached flour
6 tablespoons nonfat milk, warmed
1 tablespoon fructose
1 envelope (1 tablespoon) dry yeast
6 tablespoons low-calorie margarine (page 149)
¾ cup egg substitute (page 150), or 4 eggs
2 tablespoons raisins, plumped in water and drained
Apricot Glaze (following recipe)
2 cups fresh, unsweetened frozen and thawed, or
    water-packed canned and drained blueberries, or
    5 oranges, peeled and sectioned
¾ cup Light Whipped Topping (page 145) or
    commercial low-calorie whipped topping

Grease a nonstick 8-cup ring mold or 12 individual savarin molds and a large mixing bowl; set aside. Combine ½ cup of the flour, the milk, fructose, and yeast in a small mixing bowl and beat with a wooden spoon until smooth. Let stand until frothy, about 25 minutes. Combine the remaining flour, margarine, and egg substitute or eggs in another mixing bowl and blend well. Add the yeast mixture and beat until the dough is smooth and elastic, 3 to 4 minutes. Add the raisins and mix in well. Turn into the prepared bowl, cover, and let rise until double in bulk, 45 to 60 minutes. Punch dough down and transfer to the prepared mold(s), filling evenly. Cover and let rise in a warm place until the dough reaches the top(s) of the mold(s), about 45 minutes.

About 15 minutes before baking, preheat the oven to 375°F. Bake savarin(s) until golden and knife inserted in the center(s) comes out clean, about 20 minutes. Remove from the oven and immediately prepare the glaze.

Unmold the savarin(s) onto a serving platter and, using a sharp-tined fork, make holes over the entire surface. Spoon the syrup over the warm savarin(s) and, with a bulb baster, baste with the excess syrup every 10 to 15 minutes until all of the syrup is absorbed. Fill the center(s) with blueberries or orange segments. To serve, top each serving with 1 tablespoon whipped topping. Makes 12 servings.

Apricot Glaze

1¾ cups apricot nectar
¼ cup commercial low-sugar apricot spread
2 tablespoons cornstarch, dissolved in ¼ cup water
6 tablespoons cointreau or dark rum
1 tablespoon cognac (optional)

Combine the apricot nectar, apricot spread, and cornstarch mixture in a saucepan. Cook over low heat, stirring constantly, until the mixture thickens to a syrupy glaze. Remove from the heat and stir in the cointreau and cognac.

Each serving contains about:
179 calories
25 mg sodium
1 g fat
4 g protein
28 g carbohydrate
1 mg cholesterol

APPLE CAKE

1 cup whole-wheat pastry flour
⅓ cup fructose
1 teaspoon ground cinnamon
3 tablespoons low-calorie margarine (page 149), chilled
½ teaspoon baking soda
½ cup buttermilk
3 tablespoons egg substitute (page 150), or 1 egg
3 medium apples, peeled, and finely chopped
¼ cup ground walnuts or pecans
¾ cup low-fat apple yogurt (optional)

In a mixing bowl, combine the flour, fructose, and cinnamon. Cut in the margarine until mixture is crumbly. Remove ⅓ cup and set aside. Stir the baking soda into remaining crumbs. Beat together the buttermilk and egg substitute or egg and combine with crumb mixture. Add the apples and blend thoroughly. Turn into a lightly greased 9-inch nonstick round cake pan. Mix the reserved crumb mixture·with the nuts and sprinkle over the top. Bake in a 375°F oven for about 30 minutes, or until a knife inserted in the center comes out clean.

To serve, cut into wedges and top each serving with a dollop of yogurt, if desired. Makes 10 servings.

Each serving contains about:
  130 calories
  22 mg sodium
  3 g fat
  3 g protein
  22 g carbohydrate
  0 cholesterol

STRAWBERRY TORTE

¼ cup strawberry nectar
2 tablespoons strawberry-flavored brandy
4 cups fresh strawberries, hulled and thinly sliced
6 sheets phyllo dough
3 tablespoons low-calorie margarine (page 149), melted
2 cups Light Whipped Topping (page 145) or
    commercial low-calorie whipped topping flavored
    with 1 teaspoon pure vanilla extract

In a bowl, pour the nectar and brandy over the strawberries. Cover and refrigerate until cold, about 1 hour.

Working quickly to keep phyllo from drying out, cut each phyllo sheet into six 3½-inch circles to make 36 circles total. Brush nonstick baking sheets lightly with margarine. Place circles on baking sheets and brush tops lightly with margarine. Bake in a 400°F oven until golden, about 2 minutes. Transfer phyllo circles to paper toweling and let cool.

At serving time, gently spread all but 6 of the circles with about 1 tablespoon of whipped topping. Place 1 filled circle on each of 6 individual dessert plates. With a slotted spoon, spoon 1 tablespoon of the strawberry mixture over each. Repeat layering with remaining filled circles and strawberry mixture. Top with unfilled circles.

Spoon remaining strawberry mixture on the plates. Serve immediately. Makes 6 servings.

NOTE: For information on working phyllo dough, refer to page 76.

Each serving contains about:
  164 calories
  29 mg sodium
  3 g fat
  3 g protein
  25 g carbohydrate
  0 cholesterol

STRAWBERRY-GLAZED CHEESECAKE

¼ cup ground walnuts
1 cup fine wheatmeal biscuit or graham cracker crumbs
1 tablespoon low-calorie margarine (page 149), melted
1½ cups ricotta cheese (made from partially
      skimmed milk)
1½ cups low-fat vanilla yogurt
½ cup plus 1 tablespoon egg substitute (page 150), or
      3 eggs, beaten
1 tablespoon fresh lemon juice
3 egg whites, at room temperature
½ teaspoon cream of tartar, or
      1 teaspoon white vinegar
2 tablespoons fructose
1 cup low-fat plain yogurt
1 teaspoon pure vanilla extract
4 cups medium fresh strawberries
½ cup commercial low-sugar strawberry spread
1 tablespoon cornstarch, dissolved in ¼ cup water
¼ cup Cointreau or strawberry nectar

In a bowl, work together the walnuts, biscuit crumbs, and margarine until evenly moistened. With your fingertips or a large spoon, press onto the bottom of a 10-inch spring-form pan. Bake in a 425°F oven for 5 to 7 minutes. Remove from the oven and let cool.

In a bowl, beat together the ricotta cheese and vanilla yogurt until smooth (overmixing will cause the mixture to be too liquid). Stir in the egg substitute or eggs and lemon juice until well blended. Beat the egg whites at low speed until foamy. Add the cream of tartar and beat at medium speed until soft peaks form. Add 1 tablespoon of the fructose and beat at high speed until stiff, glossy peaks form. Stir ½ cup of the egg whites into the cheese mixture to lighten it, then gently fold in the remaining whites. Spoon over the cooled crust and smooth the top. Bake in a 350°F oven for 40 minutes. (Cake may rise slightly and crack. It will settle, cracks will minimize, and topping will cover the cracks.) Remove from the oven and let stand at room temperature for 15 minutes.

In a small bowl, combine the plain yogurt, the remaining 1 tablespoon fructose, and the vanilla extract and blend well. Spoon the topping over the cake, starting at the center and extending to within ½ inch of the edge. Return the cake to the oven and bake at 400°F for 8 minutes. Remove from the oven, let cool, and refrigerate for at least 8 hours or, preferably, 1 day.

Several hours before serving, wash, hull, and slice the strawberries and dry completely on paper toweling. In a small saucepan, melt the strawberry spread over low heat. Remove from the heat, press through a fine sieve, and return to the saucepan. Add the cornstarch mixture and the Cointreau and cook over medium heat, stirring constantly, until thick and clear, about 4 minutes. Remove the glaze from the heat and cool to lukewarm, stirring occasionally.

Using a knife, loosen the cake from the pan and remove the spring form. Arrange the berry slices attractively on top of the cake. Spoon the glaze over the berries, allowing some to drip down the sides of the cake. Return to the refrigerator until the glaze is set. Makes 12 servings.

CALORIE-SAVING TIP: Egg whites will add "creamy" volume to souffles, mousses, and cakes. Their fluffiness creates the illusion of greater quantity. For maximum volume, separate the eggs while they are cold. Beat the egg whites when they reach room temperature. Be sure to place them in a clean bowl and use clean beaters. Any trace of fat or yolk will lower the volume of the egg whites.

Each serving contains about:
    214 calories
    82 mg sodium
    6 g fat
    10 g protein
    25 g carbohydrate
    17 mg cholesterol

FLAN

½ cup fructose
¼ cup water
1 cinnamon stick (optional)
3 eggs
1 teaspoon pure vanilla extract
2½ cups nonfat milk, scalded
1 teaspoon freshly grated lemon zest

Combine ¼ cup of the fructose, the water, and cinnamon stick on a heavy saucepan and bring to a boil, shaking pan occasionally until fructose dissolves. Boil over low heat unti the syrup turns golden brown, about 20 minutes. Divide among 6 custard cups and swirl to coat sides. Beat the eggs in a small bowl. Add the remaining fructose and the vinalla extract and continue beating until well blended. Slowly stir in hot milk (if there is any foam, strain first). Stir in lemon zest and pour an equal amount into each custard cup. Arrange the cups in a shallow baking dish. Place the baking dish in the oven and add boiling water to come halfway up sides of cups. Bake at 300°F for about 35 minutes, or until a knife inserted in the center comes out clean. Remove from baking dish and let cool, then refrigerate until ready to serve. Just before serving, dip cups briefly into hot water and invert custard onto 6 individual plates. Makes 6 servings.

NOTE: This recipe depends on the eggs for its success. If you are on a low-cholesterol diet, prepare Eggless No-Bake Flan (following recipe).

Each 5-ounce serving contains about:
132 calories
80 mg sodium
3 g fat
6 g protein
22 g carbohydrate
128 mg cholesterol

EGGLESS NO-BAKE FLAN

½ cup fructose
¼ cup water
1 cinnamon stick (optional)
3 tablespoons cornstarch
½ cup plus 1 tablespoon egg substitute (page 150)
2½ cups nonfat milk
1 teaspoon pure vanilla extract
1 teaspoon freshly grated lemon zest

Combine ¼ cup of the fructose, the water, and cinnamon stick in a heavy saucepan and bring to a boil, shaking pan occasionally until fructose dissolves. Boil over low heat until syrup turns golden brown, about 20 minutes. Divide among 6 parfait glasses and swirl to coat sides. Combine the remaining fructose and cornstarch in a saucepan. Stir in egg substitute, then gradually stir in milk. Bring to a boil over medium-high heat, stirring constantly. Boil for 1 minute. Remove from the heat and stir in vanilla extract and lemon zest. Divide among the parfait glasses. Chill. Makes 6 servings.

Each 5-ounce serving contains about:
138 calories
76 mg sodium
0 fat
5 g protein
26 g carbohydrate
3 mg cholesterol

ECLAIRS

½ cup water
¼ cup unsalted margarine
½ cup unbleached flour
3 eggs
1 cup plus 2 tablespoons Chocolate Mousse (page 58),
   Custard Sauce (page 147), Light Whipped Topping
   (page 145), or commercial low-calorie whipped
   topping
½ cup plus 2 tablespoons Carob Fudge Sauce (page 143)

Combine the water and margarine in a saucepan. Heat until the margarine melts and the water boils. Reduce the heat to low, add the flour all at once, and stir vigorously with a wooden spoon until the mixture is smooth, leaves the sides of the pan, and forms a ball, about 1 minute. Remove from the heat and add 2 of the eggs, one at a time, beating well after each addition until well blended. The batter should be smooth and shiny. Cover tightly and let stand until completely cool.

Place the dough in a pastry bag with a large plain round tip and pipe out the filling in 3-inch lengths, 3 inches apart (or do this with a spoon) on a nonstick baking sheet. Beat the remaining egg and brush the tops of the pastries with it. Drag the tines of a fork across the top of each pastry to make a design. Let the éclairs dry for at least 20 minutes before baking. (The egg wash gives a shiny glaze, providing it is allowed to dry for a while before baking the éclairs.)

Bake in a 375°F oven for 20 minutes, or until well puffed and golden. Turn off the heat, open the oven door halfway, and let the éclairs cool slowly and dry for 1 hour. They will soften and collapse if cooled too quickly.

To fill, cut each éclair in half lengthwise and fill with 2 tablespoons of mousse. Spread 1 tablespoon of carob sauce over the top and chill until ready to serve. Makes 10 eclairs.

NOTE: For the success of this recipe, it is necessary to use eggs. Egg substitute cannot be used. Individuals on extremely low-cholesterol diets should avoid this dessert.

Each éclair contains about:
   146 calories
   42 mg sodium

8 g fat
4 g protein
15 g carbohydrate
77 mg cholesterol

PROFITEROLES IN CHOCOLATE SAUCE

Treat your sweet tooth to cream puffs with a French vanilla ice cream filling. You will stay well within your calorie-and-cholesterol budget because the filling is based on nonfat evaporated milk rather than cream. A traditional cream puff registers about 300 calories per serving.

> 1 cup water
> ½ cup unsalted margarine
> 1 cup unbleached flour
> 4 eggs
> 1 egg white, lightly beaten
> 2 cups French Vanilla Ice Cream (page 121), slightly
>   softened, Light Whipped Topping (page 145),
>   flavored with 1 teaspoon pure vanilla extract, or
>   Chocolate Mousse (page 58)
> ½ cup Chocolate Sauce (page 142)
> 2 tablespoons toasted slivered blanched almonds or
>   ground pistachio nuts for garnish

Combine the water and margarine in a saucepan. Place over medium heat and cook until the margarine melts and the water comes to a boil. Reduce the heat to low, add the flour all at once, and stir vigorously with a wooden spoon until the mixture is smooth, leaves the sides of the pan, and forms a ball, about 1 minute. Remove from the heat and add the eggs, one at a time, beating well after each addition until well blended. The batter should be smooth and shiny. Cover tightly and let stand until completely cool.

Place the dough in a pastry bag fitted with a ½- to ⅝-inch plain round tip and pipe out the pastry into ¾-inch puffs on nonstick baking sheets. Leave at least 1 inch between the puffs. Use a dull knife or small spatula dipped in cold water to separate the dough from the bag tip and to cut off the tops of the pastries that may burn during baking. Brush each puff with egg white. If time allows, refrigerate the puffs on the baking sheet 30 minutes, or place in the freezer 15 minutes. Transfer directly to a preheated 425°F oven (the hot oven will give them a higher rise). Bake for 18 to 20 minutes, or until golden brown and crusty. Turn off the oven, leave the oven door ajar and let the puffs stand in the oven for about 20 minutes so that the interiors dry. Transfer to wire racks and let cool away from drafts.

Slice off tops of puffs and remove. Place the softened ice cream in a pastry bag fitted with a plain round tip and fill the puffs. Replace the tops. Heap the filled puffs in a serving dish and pour the Chocolate Sauce over them. Garnish with almonds and serve immediately, or freeze until serving time if using ice cream. Makes 30 profiteroles.

NOTE: The success of this recipe depends on eggs. Egg substitute cannot be used. Note the cholesterol content if on a low-cholesterol diet.

You can freeze the unfilled, cooled puffs. Reheat without thawing in a 375°F oven for 10 to 15 minutes. These puffs are an elegant dessert to have on hand.

Each serving (2 profiteroles) contains about:
97 calories
27 mg sodium
4 g fat
3 g protein
10 g carbohydrate
64 mg cholesterol

PHYLLO DOUGH

Phyllo (also referred to as filo, yakka, brik, malsouka) dough is a very thin pastry sheet used in the Near East. In the United States, it is most often sold in Greek or Armenian markets, but it can also be found in the frozen-food section of some supermarkets and in Italian delicatessens. It is made of flour and water (to which a small amount of salt is added), and then kneaded, allowed to rest, and stretched, a procedure almost impossible for amateurs to master. It is usually sold by the pound, with approximately 24 sheets of dough, 18 by 16 inches, per package. Each sheet has only 52 calories, a very small amount of sodium, and no added fat or cholesterol.

Phyllo dough freezes well, and will keep for several days in the refrigerator, if left in the original wrapping. Thaw frozen dough by leaving it in the refrigerator overnight. For the best results, use fresh phyllo dough, if available. When working with phyllo dough, it is important to work very quickly and to keep the sheets covered with plastic wrap and a moistened towel to prevent them from drying out.

BAKLAVA

¾ pound shelled pistachio nuts, ground
1 tablespoon fructose
¾ teaspoon ground cinnamon
1½ tablespoons rose water
18 sheets (¾ pound) phyllo dough
½ cup low-calorie margarine (page 149), melted
Rose Water Syrup (following recipe)
35 whole cloves

Combine the pistachio nuts, fructose, cinnamon, and rose water in a small bowl. Using half the phyllo sheets (cover the remaining sheets with plastic wrap and a moist towel to prevent them from drying out), place 3 sheets in the bottom of a lightly greased 9-by-13-inch baking sheet. Brush with some of the margarine. Add 3 more sheets and brush with margarine. Sprinkle evenly with nut filling. Lay the remaining sheets over the nut filling, brushing after every third sheet and brushing the top sheet. Cut baklava on the diagonal at 1½-inch intervals to form 35 diamond shapes.

Bake the baklava in a 400°F oven for 25 minutes, or until golden. Remove from oven and place on wire rack to cool. Drizzle Rose Water Syrup evenly over the top and allow to soak several hours. Stud each diamond-shaped piece with a whole clove. Makes 35 servings.

NOTE: Phyllo dough and rose water are available at Middle Eastern grocery stores and gourmet food shops. For information about working with phyllo dough, refer to page 76.

I thank Chef Mo Ezzani of Yemen for developing this recipe.

Rose Water Syrup

1 cup water
½ cup fructose
1 tablespoon fresh lemon juice
1 teaspoon rose water or rum extract

Combine the water and fructose in a small saucepan. Bring to a boil and boil about 20 minutes, or until syrupy. Stir in the lemon juice and rose water.

Each serving contains about:
99 calories
1 mg sodium
5 g fat
2 g protein
11 g carbohydrate
0 cholesterol

FRUIT TURNOVERS

12 sheets (½ pound) phyllo dough
1 recipe Apple-Raisin-Nut Fruit Filling (page 107),
    Cherry Fruit Filling (page 106), or
    Blueberry Fruit Filling (page 106)
½ cup low-calorie margarine (page 149), melted

With a sharp knife, cut the phyllo dough into 48 strips each 2 inches wide and 18 inches long. Cover the strips with plastic wrap and then a moistened towel to prevent them from drying out. Remove 1 strip at a time to fill. Place 1 teaspoon filling at end of the strip and fold the corner over to form a triangle. Continue folding the dough in triangles, down the full length of the strip, to make a multilayered turnover. Brush each turnover on all sides with the margarine, using the margarine to seal any loose ends of dough. Place the filled turnovers, seam side down, ½ inch apart on a nonstick baking sheet. Keep filled turnovers covered with plastic wrap until ready to bake. Bake in a 400°F oven for 20 minutes, or until crisp and golden. Makes 48 turnovers.

NOTE: For information about working with phyllo dough, refer to page 76.

Each apple-raisin-nut turnover contains about:
    34 calories
    1 mg sodium
    1 g fat
    0 protein
    5 g carbohydrate
    0 cholesterol

Each cherry turnover contains about:
    31 calories
    0 sodium
    0 fat
    0 protein
    6 g carbohydrate
    0 cholesterol

Each blueberry turnover contains about:
    30 calories
    0 sodium
    0 fat
    0 protein
    5 g carbohydrate
    0 cholesterol

FRUIT STRUDEL

    8 sheets phyllo dough
    ⅓ cup low-calorie margarine (page 149), melted
    1 cup Apple-Raisin-Nut Fruit Filling (page 107),
        Cherry Fruit Filling (page 106), or Blueberry Fruit
        Filling (page 106)

Lightly brush a 17-by-11½-inch nonstick baking sheet with melted margarine. Place 2 sheets of phyllo dough in the bottom of the baking sheet and lightly brush with margarine. Add 2 more sheets, brush with margarine, and continue in the same manner with the remaining 4 sheets. Spread the filling along one long edge lengthwise, and roll the dough up as tightly as possible, like a jelly roll. Bake, seam side down, in a 400°F oven for 25 minutes, or until golden brown. Transfer to a wire rack to cool slightly. With a serrated-edged knife, cut on the diagonal into 16 pieces. To store, cover and refrigerate. To serve, reheat at 375°F for 5 to 10 minutes, or until crisp. Phyllo dough becomes soggy when cool. It is necessary to reheat to retain the crisp texture. Makes 16 servings.

NOTE: For information about working with phyllo dough, refer to page 76.

Each piece of apple-raisin-nut strudel contains about:
72 calories
1 mg sodium
2 g fat
0 protein
11 g carbohydrate
0 cholesterol

Each piece of cherry strudel contains about:
89 calories
1 mg sodium
1 g fat
0 protein
12 g carbohydrate
0 cholesterol

Each piece of blueberry strudel contains about:
86 calories
1 mg sodium
1 g fat
0 protein
11 g carbohydrate
0 cholesterol

The Magic of Meringues

MOCHA-ALMOND ICE CREAM IN
MERINGUE SHELLS WITH
CHOCOLATE SAUCE

3 egg whites, at room temperature
½ teaspoon cream of tartar, or
   1 teaspoon white vinegar
1 teaspoon almond extract
1 cup fructose or table sugar (sucrose)
Cornstarch
3 cups Mocha-Almond Ice Cream (page 121)
6 tablespoons Carob Fudge Sauce
   (page 143, optional)

Beat the egg whites at low speed until foamy. Add the cream of tartar and almond extract and beat at medium speed until soft peaks form. Add the fructose, ¼ cup at a time, and beat at high speed until stiff, glossy peaks form.

Line 2 heavy baking sheets with aluminum foil. Sift a thin layer of cornstarch over the foil. Using a 3 inch in diameter custard cup, drinking glass, or cookie cutter as a guide, mark 3 circles 1 inch apart on each baking sheet. Spoon three-fourths of the egg whites into a pastry bag fitted with a plain round tip. Starting in the center of each circle, pipe out 6 meringue disks in a tight concentric pattern to completely cover the circles. Change to the flute tube, add the remaining egg whites to the bag, and pipe out a decorative edge on the border of each circle. (If you do not have a pastry bag, with a spoon, form mounds about 3 inches in diameter, placing them about 1½ inches apart. Make a hollow in the center of each meringue to make nestlike forms.)

Bake the meringues in a 180°F oven until dry and firm, but not colored, about 1¾ hours. Remove from the oven, let cool, and remove from the baking sheets.

To serve, place a meringue shell on each of 6 dessert plates, set a ball of ice cream in each, and top with 1 tablespoon carob sauce, if desired. Makes 6 servings.

NOTE: Some attractive alternate flavor combinations for meringue shells:

Raspberry Cream Sherbet (page 127) with Raspberry Sauce
    (page 141)
Apple Ice Cream (page 123) with Apricot Sauce (page 141)
Coffee Bean Ice Cream (page 126) with Maple-Walnut
    Cream (page 140)
Peach Ice Cream (page 124) with Apricot Sauce (page 141)
Strawberry Ice Cream (page 125) with Strawberry Sauce (page 141)
Chocolate Mousse (page 58) with Chocolate Sauce (page 142)
Glazed sliced strawberries, kiwis, peaches, or nectarines
    (page 63) with low-fat fruit-flavored yogurt of choice

Each serving without sauce contains about:
    284 calories
    125 mg sodium
    5 g fat
    10 g protein
    55 g carbohydrate
    5 mg cholesterol

STRAWBERRY MOUSSE TORTE

3 egg whites, at room temperature
½ teaspoon cream of tartar
1 cup fructose or table sugar (sucrose)
Cornstarch
Strawberry Mousse (following recipe)
2 cups fresh strawberries
1 cup strawberry nectar
1 tablespoon cornstarch

The Magic of Meringues   83

Beat the egg whites at low speed until foamy. Add the cream of tartar and beat at medium speed until soft peaks form. Add ¾ cup of the fructose, 1 tablespoon at a time, and beat at high speed until stiff, glossy peaks form. Fold in the remaining fructose. Line 2 heavy baking sheets with aluminum foil. Sift a thin layer of cornstarch over the foil. Using an 8-inch plate or cake pan as a guide, mark a circle on each sheet. Spoon seven-eighths of the egg whites into a pastry bag fitted with a plain round tip. Starting in the center of each circle, pipe out 2 meringue disks in a tight concentric pattern to completely cover the circles. Change to a fluted tube, add remaining egg whites, and pipe a decorative edge on the border of 1 of the circles. Bake the meringues in a 180°F oven until they are dry and firm, but not colored, about 1¾ hours. Remove from the oven and let cool, then remove from the baking sheets.

Several hours before serving, place the plain meringue on a serving platter. Invert the mousse onto the meringue and remove the spring-form pan. Place in the freezer.

Reserve 1 large strawberry and hull and halve the remaining berries. Carefully overlap the halved berries in an attractive circular pattern on the meringue with the decorative edge. Place the whole berry in the center. In a small saucepan, combine the strawberry nectar and the cornstarch, stirring until the cornstarch dissolves. Cook over medium heat, stirring constantly, until the mixture thickens and becomes glossy. Paint the berry halves with the glaze. Place the berry-topped meringue on a wire rack, set over a tray or baking sheet, and refrigerate.

To serve, slide the glazed meringue over the mousse. Let stand at room temperature for 10 minutes before cutting and serving. Makes 12 servings.

Strawberry Mousse

½ cup fructose
¼ cup water
3 egg whites, at room temperature
Pinch of cream of tartar
2 cups Light Whipped Topping (page 145) or
    commercial low-calorie whipped topping
2 tablespoons Kirsch or strawberry nectar
1 cup fresh strawberries, puréed and strained

Place the fructose in a small heavy saucepan. Add the water and cook over low heat until the fructose melts, shaking the pan occasionally. Increase the heat and cook without stirring until the fructose becomes syrupy. In a mixing bowl, beat the egg whites at low speed until foamy. Add the cream of tartar and beat at high speed until stiff, glossy peaks form. Gradually add the fructose syrup and continue beating until the mixture is cool and thick, about 25 minutes. Stir one-fourth of the whipped topping into the egg whites, then gently fold in remaining topping and Kirsch. Cover and freeze for 2 hours. Stir in the strawberry purée. Pour the mixture into an 8-inch spring-form pan, cover tightly, and freeze at least 4 hours.

Each serving contains about:
    141 calories
    39 mg sodium
    1 g fat
    3 g protein
    32 g carbohydrate
    0 cholesterol

FLOATING ISLAND

Dramatic, yet simple—light and lovely cold meringue floating on a custard sauce.

    ½ cup egg substitute (page 150), or
        4 egg yolks, beaten
    1½ tablespoons cornstarch, dissolved in
        1 tablespoon water (if using egg substitute)
    ¾ cup plus 1 tablespoon fructose
    2½ cups nonfat milk
      3 egg whites, at room temperature
    ½ teaspoon cream of tartar
      1 tablespoon pure vanilla extract
    1½ tablespoons dark rum or bourbon whiskey
      2 tablespoons low-calorie margarine (page 149)
      1 tablespoon ground toasted hazelnuts or
        nuts of choice for garnish (optional)

In a medium saucepan, whisk together the egg substitute or yolks, cornstarch (omit cornstarch if using yolks), and 1 tablespoon of the fructose. Set the mixture aside.

In a heavy skillet, heat the milk over low heat. Adjust the heat so that the milk barely simmers. Beat the egg whites at low speed until foamy. Add the cream of tartar and beat at medium speed until soft peaks form. Add 1 teaspoon of the vanilla extract and gradually adding the remaining fructose, ¼ cup at a time, beat at high speed until stiff, glossy peaks form. Using a small scoop (2-tablespoon size) or a large spoon, scoop out the egg whites, form them as nearly as possible into ball shapes, and drop them in the milk to poach for 3 minutes, turning them once during the cooking time. Drain on paper toweling and continue until all the egg whites have been used (makes about 18 balls).

Strain the milk through a fine strainer, then pour into the reserved egg mixture, mixing briskly. Cook over medium heat, stirring constantly, until the mixture begins to thicken and coats the back of a spoon. Remove from the heat and stir vigorously to cool, beating in the remaining vanilla extract, the rum, and margarine. Pour the sauce into a large, shallow glass serving bowl and arrange the meringue balls on top. Chill thoroughly.

To serve, divide the meringue balls among 6 individual dessert dishes, spoon the sauce around the balls, and sprinkle with nuts, if desired. Makes 6 servings.

Each serving contains about:
    109 calories
    98 mg sodium
    1 g fat
    7 g protein
    8 g carbohydrate
    3 mg cholesterol

Normandy Pancakes

Chocolate-Dipped Fresh Fruits, from left: figs, strawberries, apricot halves (bottom) and nectarine wedges (top), grape clusters, and cherries

From left: Peach Mousse, Strawberry Mousse, and Chocolate Mousse

HEAVENLY MERINGUE TART

1 teaspoon low-calorie margarine (page 149)
3 egg whites, at room temperature
1 cup fructose
3 tablespoons cold water
1 tablespoon cornstarch
1 teaspoon pure vanilla extract
½ teaspoon cream of tartar
1 cup Light Whipped Topping (page 145) or
    commercial low-calorie whipped topping
4 kiwis, peeled and sliced, or 2 cups fresh strawberries,
    hulled and sliced, or other fresh fruit of choice

Prepare an 8-inch spring-form pan by cutting a circle of waxed paper to fit the bottom. Cut a strip of waxed paper long enough to line the sides of the pan and about 2 inches wider than its depth. Line the pan and lightly grease the paper.

In a large bowl, beat the egg whites at medium speed until soft peaks form. Gradually adding the fructose, continue to beat until fructose is thoroughly incorporated. Add the water and beat well, then beat in the cornstarch. Add the vanilla extract and cream of tartar and beat at high speed until stiff, glossy peaks form. Dip your hand into cold water and shake over the prepared pan. Turn the meringue into the pan and spread evenly over the bottom with a spatula. (The top should be fairly even.) Bake in a 350°F oven for 15 minutes. Check meringue to see if it has begun to rise. If so, turn the oven off and let set for 1 hour, if the oven retains heat well. If the oven does not retain heat well, reduce the temperature to 175°F after the first 15 minutes and bake for 1 hour longer. If the meringue has not risen, bake another 10 to 15 minutes at 250°F and then turn the oven off for 1 hour. Remove from the oven and let cool, then remove from the pan.

Place the meringue on a serving platter and spread the whipped topping evenly over it. Attractively arrange the sliced fruit on the topping. Makes 10 servings.

CALORIE-, CHOLESTEROL-, AND SALT-SAVING TIP: Meringues are the calorie-, cholesterol-, and salt-watchers' dream come true. Beaten egg whites hold their volume best when fructose is gradually added in small amounts. For best results, add no more than 1 tablespoon at a time to the whites and beat well after each addition, so the fructose is thoroughly absorbed.

Each serving contains about:
  99 calories
  23 mg sodium
  1 g fat
  2 g protein
  21 g carbohydrate
  0 cholesterol

APPLE MERINGUE PIE

2 tablespoons low-calorie unsalted margarine (page 149)
3 pounds McIntosh apples, peeled, cored, and quartered
½ cup commercial low-sugar apricot spread
  Grated zest of 1 large orange or lemon
¼ cup dark rum, or ¼ cup unsweetened apple juice
    plus ¼ teaspoon rum extract
One 2-inch piece vanilla bean, split lengthwise, or
    1 teaspoon pure vanilla extract
1 cup unsweetened apple juice
1 cup water
3 medium Golden Delicious apples, peeled and
    thinly sliced
1 cup vanilla wafers, coarsely crushed
3 egg whites, at room temperature
½ teaspoon cream of tartar
¼ cup fructose

Melt the margarine in a heavy saucepan. Add the McIntosh apples, apricot spread, and orange zest. Cook, partially covered, over medium heat for 15 minutes, stirring occasionally. Add 2 tablespoons of the rum and increase the heat. Cook apples, uncovered, stirring frequently, until reduced to a thick purée. Remove from the heat and set aside.

Combine the vanilla bean, apple juice, and water in a second heavy saucepan. Heat to boiling. Reduce the heat and simmer, covered, about 20 minutes. Add the Golden Delicious apples and poach just until tender, 3 to 5 minutes. Drain the apples, reserving the poaching liquid.

Preheat the broiler. Spread the apple purée in an even layer in a 9-inch glass pie plate or shallow oval casserole. Cover the purée with the vanilla wafer crumbs. Sprinkle with the remaining 2 tablespoons of rum. Arrange the poached apple slices in a decorative pattern on top. Drizzle with 2 tablespoons of the reserved poaching liquid. Beat the egg whites until foamy. Add the cream of tartar and beat at medium speed until soft peaks form. Gradually adding the fructose, 1 tablespoon at a time, beat at high speed until stiff, glossy peaks form. Spoon the egg whites or pipe them with a pastry bag in a border on top of the apple slices. Bake in a 450°F oven just until meringue is browned, about 5 minutes. Cool to room temperature before serving. Makes 10 servings.

Each serving contains about:
176 calories
27 mg sodium
2 g fat
1 g protein
37 g carbohydrate
0 cholesterol

HAZELNUT MERINGUE WITH PEACHES

2 tablespoons hazelnuts, toasted and skins
    partially removed
2 tablespoons walnuts or pecans
1½ tablespoons all-purpose flour
4 egg whites, at room temperature
½ teaspoon cream of tartar
1⅓ cups fructose or table sugar (sucrose)
1 teaspoon pure vanilla extract
1½ cups Light Whipped Topping (page 145) or
    commercial low-calorie whipped topping
5 medium ripe fresh freestone peaches, or
    2½ cups unsweetened frozen and thawed or
    water-packed canned peach slices

Line 2 baking sheets with aluminum foil or parchment paper and mark two 8-inch circles on each sheet, spacing them at least 1 inch apart. In a food processor or blender, grind the nuts. Transfer to a bowl, add the flour, and mix thoroughly. Set aside.

In a large bowl, beat the egg whites at low speed until foamy. Add the cream of tartar and beat at medium speed until soft peaks form. Gradually adding the fructose, 1 tablespoon at a time, beat at high speed until stiff, glossy peaks form. Fold in nut mixture, one-third at a time. Spoon egg whites into a pastry bag fitted with a plain round tip. Starting at the center of each circle, pipe out meringue disks about ⅛ inch thick in a tight concentric pattern to completely cover the circles on the baking sheets. (If you do not have a pastry bag, use a spoon or spatula to form ⅛-inch-thick mounds.) Bake in a 250°F oven for 1 hour, or until the circles are dry and firm. Turn the oven off and leave the meringue circles in the oven for 30 minutes. Remove from the oven, let cool, then remove from the baking sheets. (If using fructose, the meringue disks will be sticky and soft.)

Fold the vanilla extract into the whipped topping. If using fresh peaches, immerse them in a bowl of boiling water for 30 seconds, remove, peel, pit and thinly slice. If using canned or frozen peaches, drain and dry thoroughly. In a mixing bowl, fold the peaches into three-fourths of the whipped topping. Cover and refrigerate. Cover the remaining topping and refrigerate.

Place 1 meringue circle on a serving plate. Spread one-third of the peach mixture over the top. Repeat twice, ending with the fourth meringue. Spread remaining whipped topping over the top. Serve immediately. Makes 12 servings.

DECORATION VARIATION: Put 2 tablespoons semisweet chocolate or carob chips in the top pan of a double boiler placed over simmering water and melt, stirring constantly, until satiny and smooth. Remove from the heat. With a small paint brush or flat-bladed knife, paint one side of each of 6 washed and dried leaves with stems (any variety, about 2½ inches long and 1½ inches wide) with the melted chocolate. Place leaves, chocolate side up, on waxed paper and freeze until hard. Remove the leaves from the chocolate and attractively arrange the chocolate leaves on top of the torte.

FILLING VARIATION: Bananas, kiwis, strawberries, nectarines, or any fruit of choice may be substituted for the peaches.

NOTE: For directions on toasting hazelnuts, refer to page 92.

Each serving contains about:
  109 calories
  27 mg sodium
  2 g fat
  3 g protein
  22 g carbohydrate
  0 cholesterol

CHOCOLATE-GLAZED STRAWBERRRY MERINGUES

  3 egg whites, at room temperature
  ½ teaspoon cream of tartar
  1 cup fructose or table sugar (sucrose)
  1 cup fresh strawberries, hulled and sliced
  2 tablespoons strawberry-flavored liqueur or
     strawberry nectar
  ¼ cup hazelnuts, toasted, skins partially removed,
     and finely chopped
  1½ cups low-fat strawberry yogurt
  6 tablespoons Chocolate Sauce (page 142)

Mark eight 3-inch circles on the underside of a sheet of parchment paper or on a paper bag opened flat. Place on an aluminum foil–lined baking sheet. Mark eight 2½-inch circles on the underside of a sheet of parchment paper or a paper bag and place on a second aluminum foil–lined baking sheet.

Beat the egg whites at low speed until foamy. Add the cream of tartar and beat at medium speed until soft peaks form. Gradually adding the fructose, ¼ cup at a time, beat at high speed until stiff, glossy peaks form.

Fill a 16-inch pastry bag fitted with a #6 star tip with the egg whites. Starting at the center of each 3-inch circle, pipe meringue disks in tight concentric patterns to completely fill the circles. Continue piping at the edge to form a 3-inch high shell. Starting at the centers of the 2½-inch circles, pipe the remaining egg whites to form lids. Bake the shells on the center oven rack and the lids on the top oven rack for 30 minutes in a 250°F oven. Remove the lids to a wire rack to cool. Continue baking the shells 1 hour longer. Turn off the oven and cool the shells completely in the oven with the door ajar.

Meanwhile, pour liqueur over the sliced strawberries in a bowl and refrigerate for 1 hour. Fold the nuts into the yogurt. Spoon ¼ cup of the yogurt-nut mixture into each shell. Top with the berries, then with the lids. Spoon 1 tablespoon of Chocolate Sauce over each lid. Serve immediately. Makes 6 servings.

NOTE: To toast hazelnuts, first roast them on a baking sheet in a single layer at 350°F for 15 to 20 minutes. Cool and rub the skins off (some of the skin on each nut may continue to adhere). Then toast the nuts on a baking sheet in a 300°F oven until golden, shaking the pan occasionally.

Each serving contains about:
    257 calories
    57 mg sodium
    6 g fat
    5 g protein
    51 g carbohydrate
    6 mg cholesterol

PEACH CREAM MERINGUE

½ cup egg substitute (page 150), or
    1 egg plus 2 egg yolks
⅓ cup fructose
½ cup unbleached flour, sifted
1 cup plus 2 tablespoons nonfat milk,
    boiled with 1 vanilla bean, pierced, or
    1 teaspoon pure vanilla extract
1 cup peach nectar
2 tablespoons low-calorie margarine (page 149)
1 cup unsweetened apple juice
1 tablespoon Kirsch
6 ripe fresh freestone peaches, or 12 unsweetened
    frozen and thawed or water-packed canned
    peach halves, drained
3 egg whites, at room temperature
½ teaspoon cream of tartar, or
    1 teaspoon white vinegar

In a mixing bowl, beat the egg substitute or egg and yolks with 3 tablespoons of the fructose until the mixture thickens. Add the sifted flour, then very slowly stir in the boiling milk and the peach nectar. Pour the milk-flour into a saucepan and cook over low heat, stirring continuously with a wooden spoon, until it begins to boil. Remove from the heat and stir in the margarine. Pour into a 9-by-13-inch ovenproof glass serving dish. Cover and let cream cool. (It is important to cover it to avoid a skin from forming on the surface.)

If using fresh peaches, immerse them in a bowl of boiling water for 30 seconds, remove, peel, halve, and pit. Bring the apple juice and Kirsch to a boil and simmer several minutes. Add the peaches and poach them at a simmer until tender; remove from the heat and drain. Arrange the cooked peaches over the custard.

Beat the egg whites at low speed until foamy. Add the cream of tartar and beat at medium speed until soft peaks form. Gradually adding the remaining fructose, 1 tablespoon at a time, beat at high speed until stiff, glossy peaks form.

Cover the peaches with the egg whites, bringing them down to the edges of the dish. Make decorative swirls on the top with the back of a spoon. Bake in a 400°F oven for 5 to 10 minutes to brown the meringue. Remove from the oven, let cool, and refrigerate. Serve chilled. Makes 12 servings.

CALORIE-SAVING TIP: June and July are the months for fresh peaches and nectarines. They are among the lowest in calories of the fruits. For even fewer calories, substitute 4 cups fresh strawberries, hulled and sliced.

Each serving contains about:
111 calories
34 mg sodium
0 fat
3 g protein
20 g carbohydrate
1 mg cholesterol

Cookies

There's a place for a snack in a waist-watcher's diet, too. Too much food between meals or "empty-calorie" treats will surely spoil your eating plan. But a nutritious nibble like one of these cookies that follow takes the edge off the starving feeling that may cause a weight watcher to overeat. If you "brown bag" your lunch, pack a chewy cookie for dessert. Not only is a homemade cookie tops in taste, but a packaged cookie this big has 50 to 100 more calories.

OATMEAL-RAISIN COOKIES

   1 cup unbleached flour
   ½ cup fructose
   1 teaspoon baking soda
   1 teaspoon low-sodium baking powder (page 164) or
      regular baking powder
   ½ cup low-calorie margarine (page 149)
   6 tablespoons egg substitute (page 150), or 2 eggs
   ¼ cup low-fat vanilla yogurt
   1 teaspoon maple extract
   2 cups quick-cooking rolled oats
   ½ cup raisins

In a mixing bowl, stir together flour, fructose, baking soda, and baking powder. Add margarine, egg substitute or eggs, yogurt, and maple extract and beat well. Stir in rolled oats and raisins. Chill. Drop by heaping teaspoonfuls onto nonstick baking sheets. Bake in a 375°F oven for 8 to 10 minutes. Transfer cookies to wire racks to cool. Makes 6 dozen cookies.

Each cookie contains about:
  30 calories
  3 mg sodium
  0 fat
  1 g protein
  5 g carbohydrate
  0 cholesterol

BISCUIT TORTONI

  2 tablespoons Amaretto liqueur
  2 tablespoons peach nectar
  1 teaspoon unflavored gelatin
  ½ cup egg substitute (page 150), or 4 egg yolks
  ¼ cup water
  ¼ cup fructose
  1 cup Light Whipped Topping (page 145) or
      commercial low-calorie whipped topping
  ½ cup chopped toasted almonds
  ¼ cup crushed vanilla wafers
  1 tablespoon sliced toasted almonds for garnish

In a small saucepan, combine the liqueur, peach nectar, and gelatin and let stand until gelatin softens. Place the mixture over low heat, stirring until gelatin dissolves, about 2 to 3 minutes.

Beat the egg substitute or egg yolks in a large bowl and set aside. Combine the water and fructose in a medium saucepan and bring to a boil over medium heat, stirring until fructose dissolves. Reduce the heat and cook syrup for 10 minutes. With mixer set at low speed, slowly add hot syrup to egg substitute in a steady stream, beating until well blended. Add the gelatin mixture and continue beating until thick, about 6 minutes. Let cool. Gently fold whipped topping, chopped almonds, and vanilla wafers into mixture. Spoon into 12 foil-lined paper cups. Cover and chill.

Before serving, decorate with sliced almonds. Makes 12 servings.

Each serving contains about:
  79 calories

19 mg sodium
4 g fat
3 g protein
8 g carbohydrate
0 cholesterol

ORANGE CRESCENT COOKIES

1 cup unbleached flour
¼ teaspoon low-sodium baking powder (page 164) or
    regular baking powder
⅓ cup low-calorie margarine (page 149)
¼ cup fructose
1 tablespoon orange-flavored liqueur
2 teaspoons freshly grated orange zest
½ cup finely chopped pecans
2 tablespoons commercial low-sugar orange
    marmalade spread (optional)

Sift together the flour and baking powder. In a small mixing bowl, cream together the margarine and fructose. Stir in the liqueur and orange zest. Then stir in the flour mixture and pecans. Cover and chill for 1 hour, or until firm.

Cut off small pieces of dough and, with floured hands, form into ¾-inch balls. Roll each ball into a 2½-inch-long rope. Arrange the ropes in crescent shapes on nonstick baking sheets. Bake in a 350°F oven for 15 minutes, or until browned on the bottom. Transfer cookies to wire racks to cool.

In a small saucepan, melt the orange marmalade spread over low heat, then brush it on the cookies, if desired. Makes 30 cookies.

Each cookie contains about:
40 calories
0 sodium
2 g fat
0 protein
5 g carbohydrate
0 cholesterol

DELICES WITH FRUIT

10 dried apricots
½ cup raisins
2 large apples, coarsely chopped
1 cup low-calorie margarine (page 149)
⅓ cup fructose
1¼ cups unbleached four, sifted
½ cup ground almonds

In a food processor or blender, combine the apricots, raisins, and apples and blend until smooth. Cover and refrigerate at least 2 hours to allow the flavors to blend. In a mixing bowl, cream together the margarine and fructose. Add the flour and almonds and mix well. Cover and chill until firm, about 2 hours.

Cut off small pieces of dough and, with floured hands, roll into ¾-inch balls. Place on nonstick baking sheets. With a lightly floured thumb, make an indentation in each ball, flattening it. Fill each indentation with a teaspoonful of fruit filling. Bake in a 350°F oven for 10 to 12 minutes, or until browned on the bottom. Transfer cookies to wire racks to cool. Makes 4 dozen cookies.

CALORIE-, CHOLESTEROL-, SODIUM- AND FAT-SAVING TIP: You will lower calories, cholesterol, sodium, and fat in any recipe calling for butter by using low-calorie margarine (my version, page 149, or commercial). Sodium can be lowered further if you use unsalted margarine when making it.

NOTE: Apricot, orange marmalade, strawberry, or any commercial low-sugar spread of choice may be substituted for the apricot-raisin-apple filling. Simply fill each indentation with a teaspoonful of the spread of choice.

Each cookie contains about:
37 calories
1 mg sodium
1 g fat
0 protein
7 g carbohydrate
0 cholesterol

CHOCOLATE-PECAN COOKIES

       3 egg whites, at room temperature
   ½ teaspoon cream of tartar, or 1 teaspoon vinegar
       1 teaspoon almond extract
       1 cup fructose or table sugar (sucrose)
       3 tablespoons unsweetened cocoa or carob powder
   2½ tablespoons pecans, ground

Beat the egg whites at medium speed until soft peaks form. Add the cream of tartar and almond extract and beat at high speed until stiff, glossy peaks form. In a bowl, sift together fructose and cocoa. Add fructose-cocoa mixture to egg whites, ¼ cup at a time, beating after each addition. Fold in pecans. Drop by heaping teaspoonfuls onto foil-lined baking sheets (cookies can be placed very close together) and bake in a 250°F oven for 30 minutes. Cookies should be dry and firm. Turn off the oven and leave the cookies in the oven for 30 minutes. Remove from the oven and let cool on the baking sheet. Makes 40 cookies.

   Each cookie contains about:
       21 calories
       4 mg sodium
       0 fat
       0 protein
       5 g carbohydrate
       0 cholesterol

CHOCOLATE CHIP COOKIES

       3 egg whites, at room temperature
   ½ teaspoon cream of tartar, or 1 teaspoon white vinegar
       1 teaspoon pure vanilla extract
       1 cup fructose or table sugar (sucrose)
   ½ cup mini semisweet chocolate or carob chips

Beat the egg whites at medium speed until soft peaks form. Add the cream of tartar and vanilla extract and beat at high speed until stiff, glossy peaks form. Add the fructose, ¼ cup at a time, beating after each addition. Fold in the chocolate chips. Drop by heaping tea-spoonfuls onto a foil-lined baking sheet (cookies can be placed very close together) and bake in a 250°F oven for 30 minutes. Cookies should be dry and firm, not colored. Turn off the oven and leave the cookies in the oven for 30 minutes. Remove from the oven and let cool on the baking sheet. Makes 40 cookies.

CALORIE-SAVING TIP: Carob has a milder flavor than chocolate; thus it requires less sweetening and as a result has fewer calories.

Each cookie contains about:
  29 calories
  4 mg sodium
  1 g fat
  0 protein
  6 g carbohydrate
  0 cholesterol

RAISIN-NUT COOKIES

These cookies are a bargain at only 26 calories each, and they are low in sodium and cholesterol, too.

  3 egg whites, at room temperature
  ½ teaspoon cream of tartar, or 1 teaspoon white vinegar
  1 teaspoon maple extract
  1 cup fructose or table sugar (sucrose)
  ¼ cup raisins
  ¼ cup walnuts or pecans, chopped

Beat the egg whites at medium speed until soft peaks form. Add the cream of tartar and maple extract and beat at high speed until stiff, glossy peaks form. Add the fructose, ¼ cup at a time, beating after each addition. Fold in the raisins and nuts. Drop by heaping tea-spoonfuls onto a foil-lined baking sheet (cookies can be placed very close together) and bake in a 250°F oven for 30 minutes. Turn off oven and leave the cookies in the oven for 30 minutes. Cookies should be dry and firm, but not colored. Remove from the oven and let cool on the baking sheet. Makes 42 cookies.

NOTE: Chopped dried apples, apricots, dates, or other dried fruit of choice may be substituted for the raisins.

Each cookie contains about:
26 calories
4 mg sodium
0 fat
0 protein
6 g carbohydrate
0 cholesterol

LEAF COOKIES

½ cup low-calorie margarine (page 149)
¾ cup fructose
3 tablespoons egg substitute (page 150), or 1 egg
1½ teaspoons almond extract
1¾ cups unbleached flour
1 teaspoon baking soda
1 teaspoon low-sodium baking powder (page 164) or regular baking powder

In a large bowl, cream together the margarine and fructose. Add the egg substitute or egg and almond extract and beat until blended. Beat in flour, baking soda, and baking powder. Cover and chill in the freezer for 30 minutes.

With floured hands, divide the dough into thirds. Pat each third into a circle between 2 sheets of waxed paper, then roll out about ¼ inch thick. Chill the dough for about 2 hours, or until firm enough to cut out cookies. Using a floured, large leaf-shaped cookie cutter or homemade cardboard stencil (if using stencil, trace shape with tip of small knife), cut out cookies. Transfer cookies to nonstick baking sheets. Gather scraps into a ball and then roll out between 2 sheets of waxed paper. If this dough becomes difficult to work with, chill in freezer before attempting to cut out cookies. With a butter knife, press a vein pattern into each cookie.

Bake in a 375°F oven for 5 to 8 minutes, or until golden brown. Transfer to wire racks to cool. Makes 36 cookies.

Each cookie contains about:
    49 calories
    13 mg sodium
    0 fat
    0 protein
    9 g carbohydrate
    0 cholesterol

BOYSENBERRY BARS

½ cup low-calorie margarine (page 149)
¼ cup fructose
3 tablespoons egg substitute (page 150), or 1 egg
½ teaspoon pure vanilla extract
1 cup unbleached flour
1 cup commercial low-sugar boysenberry spread
½ cup ground pecans or walnuts

In a bowl, cream together the margarine and fructose. Beat in the egg substitute and vanilla extract until well blended. Add the flour, ⅓ cup at a time, to the margarine mixture, blending well after each addition. With a spatula, pat the dough evenly in a shallow nonstick 9-by-13-inch pan. Spread the boysenberry spread over the dough and sprinkle the top with the ground nuts. Bake in a 350°F oven for 35 minutes, or until firm. Remove from the oven, cool slightly, and cut into 1-inch squares. Makes 60 squares.

NOTE: Peach, orange marmalade, strawberry, raspberry, apricot, or any commercial low-sugar spread of choice may be substituted for the boysenberry.

Each square contains about:
    25 calories
    1 mg sodium
    1 g fat
    1 g protein
    3 g carbohydrate
    0 cholesterol

PEANUT BUTTER COOKIES

⅓ cup low-calorie margarine (page 149)
½ cup fructose
3 tablespoons egg substitute (page 150), or 1 egg
1 cup low-sodium cream-style peanut butter
½ teaspoon baking soda
¼ teaspoon ground cinnamon
1 teaspoon maple extract
1 cup sifted unbleached flour

In a bowl, cream together the margarine and fructose until well blended. Beat in egg substitute or egg, peanut butter, baking soda, cinnamon, and maple extract until smooth. Add flour and stir until blended. With floured hands, form the dough into balls about ¾ inch in diameter and place on nonstick baking sheets. Score each cookie in a criss-cross pattern with fork tines to flatten. Bake in a 375°F oven for 8 to 10 minutes, or until browned. Transfer cookies to wire racks to cool. Makes 70 cookies.

Each cookie contains about:
34 calories
4 mg sodium
2 g fat
1 g protein
3 g carbohydrate
0 cholesterol

FRUIT BARS

½ cup low-calorie margarine (page 149), melted
12 sheets (½ pound) phyllo dough
1 recipe Cherry Fruit Filling, Blueberry Fruit
    Filling, or Apple-Nut-Raisin Fruit Filling
    (following recipes)

Lightly grease the bottom of a 9-by-13-inch baking sheet with some of the margarine. Place 2 sheets of phyllo dough on the baking sheet and lightly brush with margarine. Top with 2 more sheets, brush with margarine, and repeat with 2 more sheets. Spread the filling on the phyllo dough evenly. Lay 2 more sheets on top of the filling, brush with margarine, and repeat with the remaining 4 sheets. With a sharp knife, cut the layered phyllo on the diagonal at 1½-inch intervals to form 48 diamond shapes. Bake in a 400°F oven for 25 minutes, or until golden brown. Transfer to wire racks to cool.

These bars are best eaten just after they have cooled. To store, cover and refrigerate. Reheat before serving in a 375°F oven for 5 to 10 minutes, or until crisp. Makes 48 bars.

CALORIE-, FAT-, SODIUM-, AND CHOLESTEROL-SAVING TIP: You will reduce calories, fat, sodium, and cholesterol by using low-calorie margarine (page 149).

NOTE: For information about working with phyllo dough, refer to page 76.

Each cherry fruit bar contains about:
    31 calories
    0 sodium
    0 fat
    0 protein
    6 g carbohydrate
    0 cholesterol

Each blueberry fruit bar contains about:
    30 calories
    0 sodium
    0 fat
    0 protein
    5 g carbohydrate
    0 cholesterol

Each apple-raisin-nut fruit bar contains about:
    33 calories
    1 mg sodium
    1 g fat
    0 protein
    5 g carbohydrate
    0 cholesterol

FRUIT FILLINGS

Cherry Fruit Filling

1 (16-ounce) can unsweetened Queen Anne cherries
1 tablespoon cornstarch
¼ cup reserved cherry juice
⅓ cup plus 1 tablespoon fructose
¼ teaspoon almond extract

Drain the cherries, reserving ¼ cup of the juice. In a saucepan, dissolve the cornstarch in the reserved juice. Add the fructose, almond extract, and cherries. Bring the mixture to a boil over medium heat and boil about 2 minutes, stirring constantly. Remove from the heat and cool slightly.

Blueberry Fruit Filling

2 tablespoons cornstarch
½ cup water
¼ cup fructose
¼ teaspoon ground cinnamon
⅛ teaspoon fresh finely grated lemon zest
2 cups fresh, unsweetened frozen and thawed, or
    water-packed canned and drained blueberries

In a saucepan, dissolve the cornstarch in the water. Add the fructose, cinnamon, lemon zest, and blueberries. Cook, stirring, over low heat until mixture comes to a boil. Simmer for 1 minute, stirring gently. Remove from the heat and cool slightly.

Apple-Raisin-Nut Fruit Filling

1 tablespoon low-calorie margarine (page 149)
2 medium apples (Pippin or Golden Delicious),
    peeled and chopped
½ cup unsweetened apple juice
¼ teaspoon fresh lemon juice
1 teaspoon cornstarch, dissolved in 2 teaspoons water
2 teaspoons fructose
½ teaspoon ground cinnamon
½ teaspoon pure vanilla extract
¼ teaspoon maple extract
¼ cup pecans or walnuts, chopped
3 tablespoons raisins or dried currants

In a saucepan, melt the margarine. Add the apple, apple juice, and lemon juice and mix gently. Cover and cook over low heat, stirring occasionally, until apples are just soft, about 5 minutes. Add the cornstarch mixture, fructose, cinnamon, and vanilla and maple extracts to the apple mixture. Heat, stirring, just until the mixture thickens. Remove from the heat and stir in nuts and raisins. Cool slightly.

VIP Desserts

LEMON CHEESECAKE

Substitute low-fat lemon yogurt and ricotta cheese for cream cheese and you can make a cheesecake lower in calories than you thought possible. The taste and texture will, however, be rich and creamy, just like cheesecake should be. The same-size piece of New York cheesecake would contain 200 or 300 more calories per serving.

    1 cup wheatmeal biscuit or graham cracker crumbs
    ¼ teaspoon ground cinnamon
    ¼ teaspoon freshly grated nutmeg
    2 tablespoons low-calorie margarine (page 149), melted
    1 envelope (1 tablespoon) unflavored gelatin
    2 tablespoons water, heated to boiling
    3 tablespoons fresh lemon juice
    8 ounces ricotta cheese (made from
        partially skimmed milk)
    6 tablespoons egg substitute (page 150), or 2 eggs
    ¼ cup plus 1 tablespoon fructose
    1 teaspoon pure vanilla extract
    ½ cup low-fat lemon yogurt
    2 tablespoons freshly grated lemon zest
    3 egg whites, at room temperature
    ¼ teaspoon cream of tartar
    2 ripe fresh freestone peaches, or
        1 cup water-packed canned peach slices
    Juice of ¼ lemon (if using fresh peaches)
    15 black grapes, halved and seeded

In a mixing bowl, work together the crumbs, cinnamon, nutmeg, and margarine until evenly moistened. With your fingertips or a large spoon, press the crumb mixture onto the bottom and halfway up the sides of a nonstick 8-inch spring-form pan. Refrigerate for 1 hour.

Put the gelatin in a small bowl. Add the boiling water and stir until gelatin dissolves. Add the 3 tablespoons lemon juice, mix well, and let the gelatin soften for 10 minutes. In a mixing bowl, combine the ricotta cheese, egg substitute or eggs, fructose, vanilla extract, yogurt, and lemon zest. Beat until light and fluffy. Add the gelatin mixture and beat until well blended.

Beat the egg whites at medium speed until foamy. Add the cream of tartar and beat at high speed until stiff, glossy peaks form. Stir 1 cup of the egg whites into the cheese mixture to lighten it, then gently but thoroughly fold in the remaining whites. Pour into the chilled crumb shell, smooth the top, and chill for at least 2 hours, or until the filling is set.

Place the cake on a serving platter and remove the spring-form pan. Immerse the fresh peaches in a bowl of boiling water for 30 seconds, remove, peel, halve, and pit. Thinly slice the peaches and sprinkle them with the juice of ¼ lemon. Arrange the slices in 2 overlapping concentric circles in the center of the cheese filling. Arrange the black grape halves around the edge of the cake. Makes 12 servings.

CALORIE-SAVING TIP: The lowest-calorie crackers to use for making a crumb crust are zwieback and graham crackers. Flavor them with a touch of fructose, ground cinnamon, or grated nutmeg. Presweetened crackers, such as wheatmeal biscuits, vanilla wafers, or ginger snaps, also make a good low-calorie crust. To keep the calorie count low, spread the crumbs very thinly over the bottom of a spring-form pan.

Each serving contains about:
    97 calories
    49 mg sodium
    2 g fat
    5 g protein
    12 g carbohydrate
    7 mg cholesterol

BOURMA
(Greek Nut-filled Pastry Rolls)

½ pound shelled pistachio nuts, walnuts, or
    pecans, ground
1 tablespoon fructose
¾ teaspoon ground cinnamon
1½ tablespoons rose water
12 sheets (½ pound) phyllo dough
½ cup low-calorie margarine (page 149), melted
Rose Water Syrup (following recipe)

In a mixing bowl, combine the pistachio nuts, fructose, cinnamon, and rose water. Set aside.

Unroll the phyllo dough, remove 2 sheets, and place on work surface (keep remainder of phyllo dough covered with waxed paper and a damp towel to prevent it from drying out). Lightly brush the top sheet with margarine. Sprinkle about 2 tablespoons of the nut mixture over a lengthwise half of the phyllo. Place a wooden dowel, about ¾ inch in diameter and at least 24 inches long, along the nut-filled side of the phyllo sheets. Roll the phyllo loosely around the dowel. Lay the dough, seam side down, on work surface. Lift one end of the dowel and, using your hands, gently push the dough together from each end to form a crinkled roll about 10 to 12 inches long. Slide the dough off the dowel. Insert an index finger in each end of the roll to transfer it to a nonstick jelly-roll pan about 11 by 17 inches. (Or slide the dough off the dowel directly onto the pan.) Let stand, uncovered, so phyllo dries slightly while making the remaining rolls. Repeat with remaining phyllo sheets and nut mixture. When all of the rolls are made and have dried slightly, pull the ends out accordion fashion until they touch the 11-inch sides of the pan. Pour the remaining margarine over the top and bake in a 300°F oven until lightly browned, about 35 to 40 minutes.

While the rolls are baking, make the Rose Water Syrup. Remove the rolls from the oven and drain off any excess margarine from the pan. Using a serrated-edged knife, immediately cut the rolls into pieces about 2 inches long. Pour warm syrup over warm pastries. Makes 36 pieces.

NOTE: For additional information on working with phyllo dough, refer to page 76.

CALORIE-, FAT-, AND SODIUM-SAVING TIP: Nuts are high in protein, but also very high in fat content. Pistachios have the lowest fat content, and as a result the lowest calorie content (page 177). Avoid Brazil nuts, as they have the most calories. Nuts are low in sodium if they are raw or dry roasted without salt added. Read labels to avoid hidden salt and fat.

Rose Water Syrup

1 cup water
½ cup fructose
1 tablespoon fresh lemon juice
1 teaspoon rose water or rum extract

Combine the water, fructose, lemon juice, and rose water in a saucepan, bring to a boil, and cook until a syrupy consistency, about 20 minutes. Keep warm.

Each piece contains about:
76 calories
0 sodium
4 g fat
1 g protein
8 g carbohydrate
0 cholesterol

BAVARIAN MOCHA CREAM

1 envelope (1 tablespoon) unflavored gelatin
1½ cups nonfat milk
½ cup egg substitute (page 150), or
    5 egg yolks, beaten
½ cup fructose
2 teaspoons instant decaffeinated coffee powder
1 ounce (1 square) unsweetened chocolate or
    carob, melted
¼ cup coffee-flavored liqueur
3 cups Light Whipped Topping (page 145) or
    commercial low-calorie whipped topping
2 tablespoons semisweet chocolate or carob chips
6 leaves with stems (any variety, about 2½ inches
    long and 1½ inches wide), washed and dried

Lightly grease an 8-inch spring-form pan. In a small bowl, soften the gelatin in 2 tablespoons of the milk. In a medium saucepan, combine the egg substitute or yolks and fructose. Whisk in the remaining milk. Bring the mixture to a simmer, stirring constantly. Transfer the milk mixture to a bowl and whisk in the dissolved gelatin. Stir in the coffee powder, melted chocolate, and liqueur. Stir until well blended and smooth. Refrigerate until cool.

Add 2 cups of the whipped topping to the gelatin mixture, blending completely with a whisk (mixture will be runny). Pour into the prepared spring-form pan and cover with plastic wrap. Refrigerate several hours or overnight.

Place the spring-form pan on a serving platter and remove the spring-form ring. Cover the mocha cream and return it to the refrigerator. Chill well.

Meanwhile, melt the semisweet chocolate in the top pan of a double boiler placed over simmering water, stirring constantly until satiny and smooth. Remove from the heat and, with a small paint brush or knife, paint one side of each leaf with chocolate. Place the leaves on waxed paper, chocolate side up, and freeze until hard.

Remove the chilled mocha cream from the refrigerator, place on a chilled serving platter, and remove the spring-form base. Heap the remaining whipped topping in the center of the mocha cream. Remove leaves from chocolate and attractively arrange the chocolate leaves on top. Serve immediately or chill until ready to serve. Makes 12 servings.

CALORIE-, FAT-, AND CHOLESTEROL-SAVING TIP: Use Light Whipped Topping (page 145) instead of whipped cream to reduce calories, fat, and cholesterol considerably. If using a commercial low-calorie whipped topping, compare labels for calorie and fat content.

Each ½ cup serving contains about:
113 calories
46 mg sodium
4 g fat
4 g protein
15 g carbohydrate
1 mg cholesterol

ORANGE ALASKA

6 thick-skinned oranges
2 cups low-fat orange yogurt
¼ cup orange-flavored liqueur
1 teaspoon freshly grated orange zest
2 egg whites, at room temperature
¼ teaspoon cream of tartar, or
    ½ teaspoon white vinegar
3 tablespoons fructose
¼ teaspoon pure vanilla extract
Lemon leaves for garnish

Cut off 1 inch from the top of each orange. Then cut a thin round from the base so that the orange stands upright. Using a grapefruit knife or teaspoon, gently scoop out the orange pulp. Squeeze ¼ cup juice from the pulp and strain it. Whisk the yogurt until thoroughly blended. Add the strained orange juice, liqueur, and orange zest and mix well. Spoon the yogurt mixture into the orange shells and immediately place in the freezer. Freeze until firm.

When ready to serve, beat the egg whites at low speed until foamy. Add the cream of tartar and beat at medium speed until soft peaks form. Gradually adding the fructose and vanilla extract, beat at high speed until stiff, glossy peaks form.

Spread the top of each orange shell with egg whites, completely covering the yogurt and bringing the whites well down over the edge. Place the oranges on a baking sheet.

Preheat the oven to 500°F. Place the oranges in the upper part of the oven until the meringue turns golden, not more than 3 minutes. If left too long, the yogurt mixture will liquefy.

To serve, attractively arrange the lemon leaves on 6 individual serving plates and place an orange on each. Makes 6 servings.

Each serving contains about:
   140 calories
   56 mg sodium
   1 g fat
   5 g protein
   27 g carbohydrate
   8 mg cholesterol

STRAWBERRY BOMBE CHANTILLY

2 (1-pound) packages unsweetened frozen
whole strawberries
¼ cup fructose
¼ cup orange-flavored liqueur or strawberry nectar
1 quart French Vanilla Ice Cream (page 121),
softened slightly
1½ cups Light Whipped Topping (page 145), or
commercial low-calorie whipped topping, or
¾ cup Strawberry Sauce (page 141)

Slightly thaw 6 cups (about 1½ packages) of the berries. In a food processor or blender, purée the berries, fructose, and liqueur at high speed until smooth. Pour into a shallow pan, cover, and freeze until almost firm. Spoon into a 2-quart mold, spreading evenly onto the bottom and sides to completely line the mold. Cover and return to the freezer.

Meanwhile, slightly thaw the remaining 2 cups berries and slice in half. Fold the halved berries into the softened ice cream, then pack into the center of the mold. Cover and freeze until firm.

To unmold, remove from the freezer and let stand 5 minutes. Invert onto a serving platter. Wrap a hot, damp towel around the mold and shake the mold to release the bombe. If using whipped topping, put the topping into a pastry bag and pipe it onto the top in a lattice pattern. Refreeze until topping is firm, then remove from the freezer and let stand for 10 minutes before serving. If using Strawberry Sauce, omit the whipped topping. After unmolding, let stand about 10 minutes before serving. Drizzle 2 tablespoons of the sauce over the bombe.

To serve, cut the bombe into 1-inch wedges with a sharp knife that has been dipped in hot water. Place a wedge in the center of each of 10 individual serving plates. If using Strawberry Sauce, drizzle 1 tablespoon of sauce over each serving. Makes 10 servings.

Each serving contains about:
161 calories
73 mg sodium
1 g fat
5 g protein
31 g carbohydrate
3 mg cholesterol

RASPBERRY BOMBE

While the goodness of a plain dish of ice cream or a simple sundae can't be ignored, try this elegant bombe for a dinner-party dessert. It can be prepared three to four days ahead of serving.

> 1 pint French Vanilla Ice Cream (page 121),
>   softened slightly
> ½ cup fructose
> ¼ cup water
> 3 egg whites, at room temperature
> ¼ teaspoon cream of tartar
> 2 cups Light Whipped Topping (page 145) or
>   commercial low-calorie whipped topping
> 1 tablespoon Framboise (raspberry-flavored brandy)
>   or raspberry nectar
> ¾ cup raspberries, puréed and strained
> Raspberry-Peach Sauce (following recipe)

Rinse a 6-cup ring mold and place in the freezer for about 15 minutes. Spoon the ice cream into the mold. Using the back of a spoon dipped in hot water, spread ice cream evenly to coat the interior of the mold. Freeze about 1 hour or overnight.

Place the fructose in a heavy small saucepan. Pour in the water. Place over low heat until fructose melts, shaking the pan occasionally. Increase the heat slightly and cook until fructose becomes syrupy. In a small mixing bowl, beat egg whites at medium speed until foamy. Add the cream of tartar and beat at high speed until stiff, glossy peaks form. Gradually add syrup and continue beating until mixture is cool and thick, about 25 minutes. Stir one-fourth of the whipped topping into the egg whites, then fold in the remaining topping, the Framboise, and the raspberry purée. Chill thoroughly. Pour into the mold. Tap the mold lightly on a counter to settle the filling, cover with plastic wrap, and freeze. (This can be frozen for 3 to 4 days.)

One hour before serving, invert the mold onto a large round platter. Wrap a hot, damp towel around the mold and shake it to release the bombe. Return the bombe to the freezer.

Just before serving, remove the peaches from the Raspberry Sauce with a slotted spoon. Fill the center of the bombe with the peaches and drizzle some of the sauce over the top. To serve, cut into 1-inch wedges with a sharp knife dipped in hot water. Place a wedge in the center of each serving plate, surround with peaches, and serve immediately with the remaining sauce on the side. Makes 10 servings.

Raspberry-Peach Sauce

Juice of ½ lemon (if using fresh peaches)
4 ripe fresh freestone peaches, or
    2 cups water-packed canned peach slices
1½ cups fresh raspberries
2 tablespoons Amaretto liqueur
½ teaspoon pure vanilla extract

Several hours before serving, put the lemon juice in a medium bowl. Immerse the fresh peaches in a bowl of boiling water for 30 seconds, remove, peel, pit, and thinly slice into crescents. Halve each crescent and toss them in the lemon juice to prevent discoloration. Set aside.

Combine the raspberries, liqueur, and vanilla extract in a food processor or blender and purée. Stir the purée into the peaches. Cover and chill several hours.

Each serving contains about:
    133 calories
    62 mg sodium
    2 g fat
    5 g protein
    25 g carbohydrate
    1 mg cholesterol

Cold Pumpkin Soufflé

From top: Bavarian Mocha Cream and Lemon Cheesecake

Frozen Desserts

EASY VANILLA ICE CREAM

4 cups evaporated nonfat milk
½ cup fructose
1 tablespoon pure vanilla extract

Combine the evaporated milk, fructose, and vanilla extract and stir until fructose dissolves. Chill for 1 hour, if time allows. Put in an ice cream freezer and freeze according to manufacturer's instructions. Makes 2 quarts.

CALORIE-, CHOLESTEROL-, AND FAT-SAVING TIP: To reduce calories, cholesterol, and fat considerably, use evaporated nonfat milk in place of the cream or half-half called for in recipes.

Each ½ cup serving contains about:
71 calories
74 mg sodium
0 fat
5 g protein
13 g carbohydrate
4 mg cholesterol

FRENCH VANILLA ICE CREAM

½ cup fructose
2 tablespoons unbleached flour
1 cup nonfat milk
6 tablespoons egg substitute (page 150), or
    2 eggs, beaten
3 cups evaporated nonfat milk
1 tablespoon pure vanilla extract, or
    1 vanilla bean, split lengthwise

In a saucepan, combine the fructose and flour. Gradually stir in the nonfat milk. Cook over medium-low heat, stirring constantly with a wooden spoon, until the mixture begins to thicken and comes to a boil, about 10 minutes. Gradually pour 2 tablespoons of the hot mixture into the egg substitute or eggs, stirring well with a wire whisk. Continuing to stir with a wire whisk, pour the egg mixture into the saucepan. Cook and stir for 1 minute more. Remove from the heat and gradually stir in the evaporated milk and vanilla extract. Chill for 1 hour. Put in an ice cream freezer and freeze according to manufacturer's instructions. Makes 2 quarts.

    NOTE: If using a vanilla bean, add with the nonfat milk. Remove the vanilla bean before freezing the ice cream.

Each ½ cup serving contains about:
    83 calories
    75 mg sodium
    0 fat
    5 g protein
    14 g carbohydrate
    3 mg cholesterol

MOCHA-ALMOND ICE CREAM

3 tablespoons fructose
2 tablespoons unsweetened cocoa or carob powder
1 recipe Coffee Bean Ice Cream base (page 126)
½ cup blanched almonds, slivered

In a small bowl, combine the fructose and cocoa powder and blend well. Add to the ice cream base before chilling. Put in an ice cream freezer and freeze according to manufacturer's instructions, folding nuts into mixture after processing but before hardening. Makes 1½ quarts.

Each ½ cup serving contains about:
163 calories
106 mg sodium
5 g fat
8 g protein
23 g carbohydrate
5 mg cholesterol

RICH CAROB OR CHOCOLATE ICE CREAM

¼ cup cold water
½ cup fructose
1½ cups carob or semisweet chocolate chips
2 tablespoons unsalted margarine
½ cup plus 1 tablespoon egg substitute (page 150), or
    6 egg yolks, beaten
3 cups evaporated nonfat milk
Carob Fudge Sauce (page 143) or
    Chocolate Sauce (page 142), optional

In a small saucepan, combine the water and ¼ cup of the fructose. Bring to a boil over medium heat and add the carob and margarine. Remove from the heat, cover, and let stand several minutes. Remove the lid and stir until the mixture is smooth. Transfer to a large bowl. Beat together the egg substitute or egg yolks and the remaining fructose. Beat into carob mixture. Gradually add the evaporated milk, beating constantly until blended. Chill for 1 hour, if time allows. While chilling, stir occasionally. Put in an ice cream freezer and freeze according to manufacturer's instructions. Serve, topped with 1 tablespoon Carob Fudge Sauce, if desired. Makes 1½ quarts.

Each ½ cup serving without sauce contains about:
188 calories

88 mg sodium
2 g fat
7 g protein
35 g carbohydrate
4 mg cholesterol

FRUIT ICE CREAMS

Fruit ice creams can be made by adding fruit purée and/or fruit pieces to either Easy Vanilla Ice Cream (page 120) or French Vanilla Ice Cream (page 121). If the fruit is reduced to a purée, it can be added to the ice cream base either before or during processing. If bite-sized pieces of fruit are desired in the finished ice cream, it is better to mix them in by hand at the finish of the freezing process just prior to hardening in the freezer.

APPLE ICE CREAM

 5 large apples, peeled and chopped
 Juice of 1 lemon
 ½ cup water
 ½ teaspoon ground allspice
 ¼ teaspoon ground cinnamon
 1 recipe Easy Vanilla Ice Cream base (page 120)

In a large saucepan, combine the apples, 2 tablespoons of the fructose called for in the Easy Vanilla Ice Cream recipe, lemon juice, and water. Cover and cook over medium heat, stirring frequently, until apples are very soft. Remove from the heat and let cool. Mash apples with a fork to a coarse purée (makes about 2½ cups purée). Add allspice and cinnamon and mix until well blended. Add purée to ice cream base and blend well. Chill for 1 hour. Put in an ice cream freezer and freeze according to manufacturer's instructions. Makes 3 quarts.

Each ½ cup serving contains about:
 73 calories
 50 mg sodium

0 fat
3 g protein
15 g carbohydrate
3 mg cholesterol

APRICOT OR PEACH ICE CREAM

3 pounds ripe fresh apricots or freestone peaches,
  or 12 unsweetened frozen or water-packed
  canned apricots or peaches
1 tablespoon apricot- or peach-flavored brandy, or
  2 teaspoons fresh lemon juice
½ recipe Easy Vanilla Ice Cream base (page 120)
Apricot Sauce (page 141, optional)

If using fresh apricots or peaches, immerse them in a bowl of boiling water for 30 seconds, remove, peel, pit, and cut into bite-sized pieces. If using frozen fruit, allow to thaw completely, then drain well and chop. If using canned fruit, drain well and chop.

In a food processor or blender, combine half of the fruit, the brandy, and 2 tablespoons fructose from the Easy Vanilla Ice Cream recipe. Purée briefly, to measure 3½ cups. Add peach or apricot purée to ice cream base and blend well. Chill for 1 hour. Put in an ice cream freezer and freeze according to manufacturer's instructions. Top each serving with 1 tablespoon Apricot Sauce, if desired. Makes 1 gallon.

Each ½ cup serving without sauce contains about:
  39 calories
  19 mg sodium
  0 fat
  2 g protein
  9 g carbohydrate
  1 mg cholesterol

BERRY ICE CREAM

2 cups fresh or water-packed canned and drained
    strawberries, raspberries, blueberries, or berries
    of choice, or 1 (10-ounce) package unsweetened
    frozen and thawed strawberries, raspberries,
    blueberries, or berries of choice
3 tablespoons fructose
1 tablespoon fresh lemon juice
½ recipe French Vanilla Ice Cream base
    (page 121), chilled
Raspberry Sauce (page 141, optional)

Combine the berries, fructose, and lemon juice in a food processor
or blender. Purée briefly, to measure 2 cups. Add berry purée to ice
cream base and blend well. Chill for 1 hour. Put in an ice cream
freezer and freeze according to manufacturer's instructions. Top
each serving with 1 tablespoon Raspberry Sauce, if desired. Makes
2 quarts.

    Each ½ cup serving without sauce contains about:
      56 calories
      38 mg sodium
      0 fat
      3 g protein
      11 g carbohydrate
      2 mg cholesterol

CANTALOUPE ICE CREAM

1 medium cantaloupe, peeled, seeded, and cut into
    bite-sized pieces
1 tablespoon orange-flavored liqueur
½ recipe Easy Vanilla Ice Cream base (page 120)

In a food processor or blender, combine the cantaloupe, liqueur, and
2 tablespoons of the fructose called for in the Easy Vanilla Ice Cream
recipe. Purée briefly, to measure 1½ cups. Add the cantaloupe purée
to the ice cream base and blend well. Chill for 1 hour. Put in an ice

cream freezer and freeze according to manufacturer's instructions. Makes 1½ quarts.

Each ½ cup serving contains about:
   78 calories
   77 mg sodium
   0 fat
   5 g protein
   15 g carbohydrate
   4 mg cholesterol

COFFEE BEAN ICE CREAM

   4 cups evaporated nonfat milk
   ½ cup fructose
   ¼ cup decaffeinated coffee beans, coarsely ground, or
       2½ tablespoons instant decaffeinated coffee granules
   2 tablespoons unsalted margarine
   ¼ cup plus 2 tablespoons egg substitute (page 150), or
       2 eggs, lightly beaten
   2 teaspoons unbleached flour
   Maple-Walnut Cream (page 140, optional)

In a saucepan, combine the evaporated milk, fructose, ground coffee beans, and margarine and bring to a boil over medium heat. Remove from the heat, cover, and let stand 10 to 15 minutes. Strain through a cheesecloth-lined strainer into a bowl. (If using instant coffee, bring milk, fructose, and margarine to a boil, then stir in coffee.)

In a large saucepan, blend egg substitute or eggs into flour. Stir in coffee mixture. Place over low heat, stirring constantly, until mixture begins to thicken; do not boil. Remove from the heat and let cool to room temperature. While cooling, stir often to prevent a skin from forming. Cover and refrigerate until well chilled. Put in an ice cream freezer and freeze according to manufacturer's instructions. Top each serving with 1 tablespoon Maple-Walnut Cream, if desired. Makes 2 quarts.

CALORIE-SAVING TIP: Tablespoon for tablespoon, fructose has the same number of calories as sucrose (table sugar), but you need less to sweeten a dessert to the same intensity. There is no type of sugar that is "better" for you, including honey. All crystal-type sugars, no matter what their color, have the same calorie count and contain no or very few nutrients.

Each ½ cup serving without topping contains about:
92 calories
79 mg sodium
2 g fat
5 g protein
14 g carbohydrate
4 mg cholesterol

RASPBERRY CREAM SHERBET

3 egg whites, at room temperature
¼ teaspoon cream of tartar or white vinegar
2 teaspoons unflavored gelatin
¼ cup water
1 cup Raspberry Sauce (page 141)
1 cup Light Whipped Topping (page 145) or
     commercial low-calorie whipped topping

In a mixing bowl, beat the egg whites at low speed until foamy. Add the cream of tartar and beat at high speed until stiff, glossy peaks form. In a saucepan, soften the gelatin in the water over low heat, stirring until dissolved. In a large bowl, stir the gelatin into the Raspberry Sauce. Fold the Raspberry Sauce mixture into the beaten egg whites, one-third at a time, then fold the whipped topping into the egg white mixture. Pour into a rectangular pan or freezer tray, cover, and freeze until slushy, about 1 hour. Stir or beat the mixture until it is completely smooth. Pour into a plastic container and cover tightly. Freeze until firm. Makes 2 cups.

Each ½ cup serving contains about:
26 calories
15 mg sodium
0 fat
1 g protein
5 g carbohydrate
0 cholesterol

MELON SHERBET

2 medium ripe cantaloupes, peeled, seeded, and
   coarsely chopped
3 tablespoons fructose
¼ cup evaporated nonfat milk
2 tablespoons Kirsch

In a food processor or blender, purée cantaloupe to measure 4 cups.
Transfer to a bowl. Add the fructose and stir until it dissolves. Add
the evaporated milk and Kirsch and mix well. Pour the mixture into a
rectangular pan or freezer tray and freeze, covered, until slushy,
about 1 hour. Transfer the mixture to a chilled bowl and beat until it
is completely smooth. Return the mixture to the pan and place it,
covered, in the freezer again. When the mixture is almost firm, beat it
again until creamy and light. Spoon into a plastic container and
cover tightly. Freeze the sherbet until it is almost firm.

Serve the sherbet fairly soft. If the mixture becomes too firm, place
it in the refrigerator and allow it to stand for 1 or 2 hours before serving time. To serve, spoon into dessert glasses. Makes 1½ quarts.

Each ½ cup serving contains about:
   34 calories
   12 mg sodium
   0 fat
   1 g protein
   7 g carbohydrate
   0 cholesterol

STRAWBERRY SORBET

Ripe fresh strawberries to make 3 cups of purée, plus
   1 perfect berry to decorate each serving (about
   1 pound or 3 baskets)
1½ tablespoons unflavored gelatin
1½ cups water
¼ cup fructose
Juice of 1 lemon or to taste
1 small fresh mint leaf per serving for
   garnish (optional)
Light Whipped Topping (page 145) or
   commercial low-calorie whipped topping (optional)

Choose the best ripe berries you can find and hull them (except the ones you will use to decorate each serving; refrigerate these). In a food processor blender, purée enough berries to make 3 cups of purée, then strain purée through a fine sieve.

In a small saucepan, soften the gelatin in the water for 1 minute. Add the fructose and place over low heat, stirring constantly, until gelatin dissolves. Remove from the heat and let cool. Stir in puréed strawberries and lemon juice. Turn into a bowl or freezer tray, cover, and freeze until slushy, about 1 hour. Remove from the freezer and beat mixture until it is completely smooth. Return to the freezer, covered, and freeze until almost solid. Beat again, cover, return to the freezer, and freeze until solid. Remove from the freezer and whip with an electric beater or in a food processor until smooth.

To serve, spoon into chilled stemmed parfait glasses (flutes). Decorate with a berry, a mint leaf, and a dollop of whipped topping, if desired. Makes 1 quart.

NOTE: To set 1 pint of liquid, use 1 tablespoon unflavored gelatin.

Each ½ cup serving without topping contains about:
   52 calories
   1 mg sodium
   0 fat
   1 g protein
   13 g carbohydrate
   0 cholesterol

NECTARINE SORBET WITH STRAWBERRIES

½ cup peach nectar
⅓ cup fructose
1 tablespoon candied ginger, minced
4 large ripe fresh nectarines, peeled and chopped
1 teaspoon freshly grated lemon zest
Juice of 1 lemon
1 cup Yogurt Sauce (page 145)
18 unhulled fresh strawberries

In a medium saucepan, combine the peach nectar, fructose, and ginger. Place over medium heat and cook, stirring, until fructose dissolves. Increase heat to high and boil 5 minutes. Remove from the heat and let cool to room temperature. Cover and chill thoroughly. (Syrup can be prepared a day ahead of time.) Combine the nectarines and lemon zest and juice in a food processor or blender and purée. Add cold syrup and blend well. Turn sorbet into a shallow pan, cover, and freeze.

To serve, place 3 strawberries on each dessert plate. Cut sorbet into small squares and beat in batches in a food processor or blender. Place a scoop on each of 6 dessert plates and drizzle with a strip of Yogurt Sauce. Serve immediately. Dip berries in remaining sauce before eating. Makes 12 servings.

Each ½ cup serving with sauce contains about:
74 calories
13 mg sodium
0 fat
2 g protein
18 g carbohydrate
2 mg cholesterol

GRAPE SORBET WITH LEAF COOKIES

Select only the sweetest grapes for this puréelike sorbet.

>   1 envelope (1 tablespoon) unflavored gelatin
>   ¼ cup water
>   2 tablespoons fructose
>   1¼ pounds ripe Riber grapes, seeded, puréed, and
>   strained, or 2 cups unsweetened purple grape juice
>   Juice of 1 lemon
>   12 large grape leaves or other large fresh leaves,
>   washed and dried
>   6 Leaf Cookies (page 102)

In a small saucepan, soften the gelatin in water for 1 minute. Add the fructose and place over low heat, stirring constantly, until gelatin dissolves. Remove from the heat and let cool. Stir in puréed grapes and lemon juice and mix well. Turn into a bowl or freezer tray, cover, and freeze until slushy. Beat the mixture until it is completely smooth, cover, return to the freezer, and freeze until almost solid. Beat again, cover, return to the freezer, and freeze until solid. (Makes 1½ quarts of sorbet.)

Remove from the freezer and let soften in the refrigerator for 10 to 20 minutes before serving. To serve 6, arrange 2 leaves on each of 6 individual chilled serving plates. Working quickly with a small ice cream scoop or melon baller, form a "cluster" of grape sorbet balls on top. Place a leaf cookie on each plate. Makes 6 servings.

Each ½ cup serving (with a cookie) contains about:
>   105 calories
>   18 mg sodium
>   0 fat
>   1 g protein
>   24 g carbohydrate
>   0 cholesterol

COFFEE-CHOCOLATE PIE

20 Nabisco Famous Chocolate Wafers,
    finely crushed
1 tablespoon plus 2 teaspoons low-calorie
    margarine (page 149), melted
1 quart Mocha-Almond Ice Cream (page 121),
    softened slightly
2 tablespoons Chocolate Sauce (page 142)
1 quart Rich Carob or Chocolate Ice Cream (page 122),
    softened slightly

In a mixing bowl, work together wafer crumbs and margarine until evenly moistened. With your fingertips or a large spoon, press the crumb mixture evenly over the bottom and sides of a nonstick 9-inch spring-form pan. Freeze for 1 hour.

In a food processor or with an electric beater, whip softened Mocha-Almond Ice Cream until smooth. Pour evenly into crumb crust. Cover and freeze for 1 hour. Spread Chocolate Sauce evenly over Mocha-Almond Ice Cream. Cover and freeze until firm.

In a food processor or with an electric beater, whip softened Rich Carob or Chocolate Ice Cream until smooth and pour on top of Chocolate Sauce layer. Cover and freeze for at least 6 hours or overnight.

To serve, invert the spring-form pan onto a chilled round serving platter and remove the pan. Let stand 10 minutes before slicing. Makes 12 servings.

Each serving (one-twelfth of the pie) contains about:
    211 calories
    82 mg sodium
    6 g fat
    6 g protein
    33 g carbohydrate
    3 mg cholesterol

PINEAPPLE BOMBE

3 cups graham cracker, wheatmeal biscuit, or
    vanilla wafer crumbs
2 tablespoons low-calorie margarine
    (page 149), melted
1 tablespoon fructose
1 quart French Vanilla Ice Cream (page 121),
    softened slightly
2 cups low-fat orange yogurt
1 (8-ounce) can water-packed crushed
    pineapple, drained
1½ cups Light Whipped Topping (page 145) or
    commercial low-calorie whipped topping

In a mixing bowl, work together 1½ cups of the graham cracker crumbs, the margarine, and fructose until evenly moistened. With your fingertips or a large spoon, press the crumb mixture onto the bottom and sides of a 9-cup mold, cover and freeze for 1 hour.

In a chilled bowl, beat the ice cream until smooth but not melted. Starting from the top, spread evenly inside the mold to line completely. Cover and freeze until firm, about 2 hours. Remove from the freezer and press the remaining graham cracker crumbs against the ice cream to line completely, forming a layer about ⅛ inch thick. Stir the yogurt until smooth and spread evenly over the graham cracker layer. Cover and freeze until firm, about 2 hours.

Fold the pineapple into the whipped topping. Remove the mold from the freezer and spoon the whipped topping mixture into the center. Smooth the top and freeze overnight.

To unmold, remove the freezer and let stand for 5 minutes. Invert onto a chilled serving plate. Hold a hot, damp cloth over the mold and shake the mold to release the bombe. Makes 10 servings.

Each ¾ cup serving contains about:
    177 calories
    143 mg sodium
    3 g fat
    9 g protein
    28 g carbohydrate
    7 mg cholesterol

PEACHES-AND-CREAM ICE CREAM CAKE

1 cup vanilla wafer or wheatmeal biscuit crumbs
  (about 20 vanilla wafers or 15 wheatmeal biscuits)
¼ teaspoon ground cinnamon
 Dash of ground nutmeg
2 tablespoons low-calorie unsalted margarine
  (page 149), melted
1½ quarts Peach Ice Cream (page 124),
   softened slightly
1 quart French Vanilla Ice Cream (page 121),
   softened slightly
1½ cups Apricot Sauce (page 141)

In a mixing bowl, work together the crumbs, cinnamon, nutmeg, and margarine until evenly moistened. With your fingertips or a large spoon, press the crumb mixture evenly onto the bottom and sides of a nonstick 9-inch spring-form pan. Cover and freeze for 1 hour.

In a food processor or with an electric beater, whip the Peach Ice Cream until smooth. Pour into the crumb crust, cover, and freeze for 1 hour. In a food processor with an electric beater, whip the French Vanilla Ice Cream until smooth and pour on top of the frozen Peach Ice Cream. Cover and freeze for at least 6 hours or overnight.

To serve, invert the spring-form pan onto a chilled round platter and remove the pan. Let stand 10 minutes before slicing. Top each serving with 2 tablespoons Apricot Sauce. Makes 12 servings.

Each serving (one-twelfth of the pie) contains about:
  220 calories
  118 mg sodium
  6 g fat
  10 g protein
  32 g carbohydrate
  5 mg cholesterol

FILLED CANTALOUPE A LA CREME

3 small cantaloupes
3 cups Easy Vanilla Ice Cream (page 120), softened
6 unhulled fresh strawberries for garnish
Mint sprigs for garnish

Cut the cantaloupes in half, discard the seeds, and carefully scoop out the flesh, leaving the shells intact. Rinse with cold water. Freeze the shells for 1 hour, or until they are solidly frozen.

Meanwhile, chop the scooped-out cantaloupe flesh and mix it with the ice cream. Spoon the ice cream-cantaloupe mixture into the frozen shells. Freeze the filled shells, covered with plastic wrap, until they are firm. Remove from the freezer, place each melon half on an individual serving plate, and garnish each with a strawberry and a mint sprig. Serve immediately. Makes 6 servings.

NOTE: An alternate way to prepare this dessert is to scoop the flesh out with a melon baller, then remove any remaining flesh from the skins. Chill the melon balls and freeze the shells. Just before serving, fill the melon shells with balls of Easy Vanilla Ice Cream mixed with the melon balls. Garnish as directed.

Each serving contains about:
57 calories
23 mg sodium
0 fat
1 g protein
14 g carbohydrate
0 cholesterol

PECAN ICE CREAM LOG

   ¼ cup pecans, finely chopped
   4 tablespoons unsweetened cocoa or carob powder
   8 egg whites, at room temperature
   ½ teaspoon cream of tartar
   ¾ cup fructose
   ½ cup egg substitute (page 150), or 8 egg yolks
   1 teaspoon pure vanilla extract
   Low-calorie margarine for preparing baking sheet
   1½ quarts French Vanilla Ice Cream (page 121),
      Coffee Bean Ice Cream (page 126), or
      Rich Carob or Chocolate Ice Cream (page 122)
   ¼ cup plus 2 tablespoons Chocolate Sauce (page 142)
   ¼ cup pecans, coarsely chopped (optional)

Mix the finely chopped pecans with 3 tablespoons of the cocoa powder in a small bowl and set aside. Beat the egg whites at low speed until foamy. Add the cream of tartar and beat at medium speed until soft peaks form. Gradually adding ¼ cup of the fructose, beat at high speed until stiff, glossy peaks form. In a large bowl, combine the egg substitute or egg yolks with the remaining fructose and the vanilla extract and beat until well blended. Stir in 1 cup of the beaten egg whites to lighten it, then gently fold in the reserved nut mixture alternately with the remaining whites, being careful not to overfold. Some streaks of white should show.

For easy removal, jelly-roll cakes should be baked on a 10½-by-15½-by-1-inch baking sheet. Grease the baking sheet with low-calorie margarine, then line the bottom with a strip of parchment paper or aluminum foil that extends to the edges of the pan. Lightly grease the paper with low-calorie margarine. Pour in the batter, making sure it reaches to the corners. Bake in a 375°F oven for 20 minutes. Remove from the oven and immediately loosen the edges of the cake with a thin-bladed knife. Sift the remaining cocoa powder over the surface of the cake. Invert the pan onto a clean towel and lift off the pan. Immediately peel off the paper and roll up the cake before it cools, using the towel to roll it. Later, when ready to fill it, unroll the cake, fill it, and use the towel to roll it up again.

To assemble, soften the ice cream just until it can be spread.

Spread it to within 1 inch of the long edges of the cake. Drizzle ¼ cup of the Chocolate Sauce over the top. Using the towel as an aid, roll the cake into a long cylinder. Freeze until firm. Remove from the freezer, brush with the remaining 2 tablespoons of Chocolate Sauce, and roll in the coarsely chopped pecans, if desired. Return to the freezer until firm.

To serve, remove from the freezer and place on a serving platter seam side down. Let stand at room temperature for 10 minutes. Slice on the diagonal into pieces ½ inch thick. Makes 18 servings.

Each serving contains about:
    118 calories
    77 mg sodium
    1 g fat
    6 g protein
    20 g carbohydrate
    2 mg cholesterol

Toppings and Specialty Recipes

MAPLE-WALNUT CREAM

Wonderful over Coffee Bean or Mocha-Almond Ice Cream.

½ cup commercial low-sugar maple syrup
⅓ cup cold brewed decaffeinated coffee
¼ cup walnuts or pecans, finely chopped
½ cup Light Whipped Topping (page 145) or
    commercial low-calorie whipped topping

In a small saucepan, combine the maple syrup and coffee and bring to a boil over medium heat. Remove from the heat and let cool to room temperature. Fold the cooled syrup and the nuts into the whipped topping. Makes 1¼ cups.

NOTE: Because the sauce tends to separate slightly when it stands, stir several times before serving. This sauce will keep, refrigerated, for up to 1 week.

Each tablespoon contains about:
22 calories
2 mg sodium
1 g fat
0 protein
3 g carbohydrate
0 cholesterol

APRICOT SAUCE

1 (8.5-ounce) jar low-sugar apricot spread
⅓ cup water
1 tablespoon cognac (optional)

In a small saucepan, combine the apricot spread and water. Melt over low heat, stirring frequently. Remove from the heat and stir in the cognac, if desired. Strain through a fine sieve into a small pitcher. Serve warm. Makes about 1⅓ cups.

NOTE: Strawberry, raspberry, orange marmalade, or any low-sugar spread of choice may be substituted for the apricot spread.

Each tablespoon contains about:
3 calories
0 sodium
0 fat
0 protein
1 g carbohydrate
0 cholesterol

RASPBERRY SAUCE

2 (10-ounce) packages unsweetened frozen
     raspberries, thawed
Juice of ½ lemon
2 tablespoons fructose
1 teaspoon cornstarch

In a food processor or blender, combine the undrained raspberries and lemon juice and purée. Strain through a fine sieve, pressing with the back of a spoon to remove as much liquid as possible. In a saucepan, combine the fructose and cornstarch and mix well. Stir in the strained berries. Place over medium heat and bring to a boil, stirring frequently. Reduce the heat and cook, stirring constantly, until sauce thickens. Makes 2½ cups.

NOTE: Four cups fresh strawberries or 2 (10-ounce) packages unsweetened frozen blueberries may be substituted for the raspberries.

Each tablespoon contains about:
  17 calories
  0 sodium
  0 fat
  0 protein
  4 g carbohydrate
  0 cholesterol

ORANGE WHIPPED TOPPING

This topping is delicious on any fresh fruit.

  ⅓ cup instant nonfat dry milk crystals
  ⅓ cup ice cold unsweetened orange juice
  2 tablespoons fructose

Chill a small bowl and beaters. Whip milk crystals and orange juice on highest speed until stiff, about 3 to 5 minutes. Fold in fructose. Serve at once. Makes 1 cup.

  Each tablespoon contains about:
    12 calories
    7 mg sodium
    0 fat
    0 protein
    3 g carbohydrate
    0 cholesterol

CHOCOLATE SAUCE

  2 ounces (2 squares) unsweetened chocolate or carob,
    cut into small pieces
  ¼ cup fructose
  6 tablespoons nonfat milk, scalded
  ½ teaspoon pure vanilla extract

Combine the chocolate, fructose, milk, and vanilla extract in a food processor or blender and blend until smooth. Makes ¾ cup.

NOTE: One-fourth cup semisweet chocolate or carob chips may be substituted for the unsweetened chocolate or carob; omit fructose.

Each tablespoon contains about:
 41 calories
 4 mg sodium
 3 g fat
 1 g protein
 6 g carbohydrate
 0 cholesterol

CAROB FUDGE SAUCE

½ cup carob or semisweet chocolate chips
½ cup evaporated nonfat milk

In a saucepan, combine the carob and evaporated milk. Cook over low heat, stirring constantly, until carob melts and mixture is smooth. Makes 1 cup.

Each tablespoon contains about:
 26 calories
 10 mg sodium
 0 fat
 1 g protein
 6 g carbohydrate
 0 cholesterol

GRAND MARNIER SAUCE

1 tablespoon fructose
½ teaspoon cornstarch
½ cup strawberry nectar
 Finely grated zest of ½ orange
 Finely grated zest of ½ lemon
¼ vanilla bean, split lengthwise, or
  ½ teaspoon pure vanilla extract
½ cup egg substitute (page 150), or
  4 egg yolks, lightly beaten
1½ teaspoons unflavored gelatin, softened in
  2 tablespoons cold water
1 cup Light Whipped Topping (page 145) or
  commercial low-calorie whipped topping
1 tablespoon Mandarin Napoléon liqueur or
  orange-flavored liqueur of choice
2 tablespoons Grand Marnier

Combine the fructose and cornstarch in the top pan of a double boiler and mix well. Stir in the strawberry nectar, orange and lemon zests, and vanilla bean or extract until well blended. Set over simmering water and stir constantly until mixture begins to thicken, about 5 minutes. Stir a small amount of the nectar mixture into the egg substitute or yolks, then add to pan and continue cooking, stirring constantly, until thickened, about 5 minutes. Stir in gelatin, blending thoroughly. Remove from the heat and pour through a strainer into a large bowl. Cover and chill. Fold whipped topping into chilled mixture. Add liqueur and Grand Marnier and stir until smooth. Makes 2 cups.

Each tablespoon contains about:
    13 calories
    5 mg sodium
    0 fat
    1 g protein
    1 g carbohydrate
    0 cholesterol

YOGURT SAUCE

This simple sauce complements most any fruit or sorbet.

1 cup low-fat plain yogurt
1 tablespoon honey
⅛ teaspoon ground cinnamon

Combine the yogurt, honey, and cinnamon and whisk until well blended. Makes 1 cup.

Each tablespoon contains about:
12 calories
7 mg sodium
0 fat
1 g protein
2 g carbohydrate
1 mg cholesterol

LIGHT WHIPPED TOPPING

1 teaspoon unflavored gelatin
¼ cup cold water
4 teaspoons fructose
1 teaspoon pure vanilla extract
3 tablespoons whipping cream
4 egg whites, at room temperature
½ teaspoon cream of tartar, or
    1 teaspoon white vinegar

In a small saucepan, soften the gelatin in the water for 1 minute. Add the fructose and place over medium heat, stirring until gelatin dissolves. Remove from the heat and transfer to a small bowl. Stir in vanilla extract and cream. Refrigerate until set, about 1 hour.

Beat the egg whites at low speed until foamy. Add the cream of tartar and beat at high speed until stiff, glossy peaks form. With an electric beater, beat gelatin mixture until creamy, then fold into egg whites. Refrigerate until ready to use. For the best texture, use within 1 hour. Makes 2½ cups.

Each tablespoon contains about:
  6 calories
  5 mg sodium
  0 fat
  0 protein
  1 g carbohydrate
  1 mg cholesterol

ORANGE CREAM

Serve with any fresh fruit or in éclairs (page 74) or cream puffs (page 75).

  1½ cups low-fat orange yogurt
  ¼ cup unsweetened orange juice
  1 teaspoon pure vanilla extract
  1 tablespoon orange-flavored liqueur (optional)

Combine the yogurt, orange juice, vanilla extract, and liqueur in a small bowl. Stir until blended. Refrigerate 1 hour, or until serving time. Makes 1¾ cups.

Each tablespoon contains about:
  13 calories
  6 mg sodium
  0 fat
  1 g protein
  2 g carbohydrate
  1 mg cholesterol

CUSTARD SAUCE

¾ cup egg substitute (page 150), or 4 egg yolks
1½ tablespoons cornstarch, dissolved in
     1 tablespoon water (if using egg yolks,
     omit cornstarch)
¼ cup fructose
2½ cups nonfat milk
  1 tablespoon pure vanilla extract
1½ tablespoons dark rum or bourbon whiskey
  2 tablespoons low-calorie margarine (page 149)

In a saucepan, beat together egg substitute or yolks, cornstarch (if using yolks), and fructose. Place over medium-high heat and gradually stir in milk with a wooden spoon. Bring to a boil and cook, stirring constantly, until mixture begins to thicken and coats the back of a spoon. Remove from the heat and stir in vanilla extract, rum, and margarine. Serve hot, or stir vigorously to cool and serve cold. Makes 2 cups.

Each tablespoon contains about:
  27 calories
  16 mg sodium
  0 fat
  1 g protein
  3 g carbohydrate
  1 mg cholesterol

FRUIT SPREAD

10 dried apricots
½ cup raisins
 2 large apples, cored

In a food processor or blender, combine the apricots, raisins, and apples. Blend until smooth. Refrigerate at least 2 hours to allow the flavors to blend. Makes 1¼ cups.
    CALORIE-SAVING TIP: This fruit spread is an excellent, nutri-

tious, (high in vitamin A and iron), low-calorie substitute for jams and jellies. Great on homemade breads, muffins, or crackers.

Each tablespoon contains about:
    23 calories
    1 mg sodium
    0 fat
    0 protein
    6 g carbohydrate
    0 cholesterol

SPECIAL CREAM

1½ cups ricotta cheese (made from partially skimmed milk) or low-fat cottage cheese
1½ cups low-fat vanilla yogurt

Combine the ricotta cheese and yogurt and stir until well blended and smooth (overmixing will cause the mixture to be too liquid). Let stand at room temperature for 1 hour. For best results, refrigerate at least 10 hours before using. Makes 3 cups.

CALORIE- AND FAT-SAVING TIP: Special Cream is lower in calories, fat, and cholesterol than cream and can be substituted for cream in any dessert recipe. Cream is an "empty-calorie" food because it contains mostly fat. Special Cream is a good source of protein, calcium, and riboflavin.

NOTE: This sauce will keep, refrigerated, for up to 10 days.

Each tablespoon contains about:
    15 calories
    4 mg sodium
    1 g fat
    1 g protein
    1 g carbohydrate
    3 mg cholesterol

LOW-CALORIE MARGARINE

Low-calorie margarine is essentially margarine whipped with water. To save money, make your own. It is necessary to use at least three cups of margarine to incorporate the water completely.

3 cups regular or unsalted margarine, chilled
3 tablespoons nonfat milk powder
1½ cups ice water

Place the margarine, milk powder, and water in a food processor or blender container and whip until water is well incorporated and margarine is light and fluffy. (You will need to turn the blender on and off, scraping mixture into blades when off.) Store in a covered plastic container for 2 to 3 weeks, or freeze for up to 3 months. Use as you would regular margarine. Makes about 6 cups.

NOTE: For each additional cup of margarine you wish to whip, add ½ cup water.

Each tablespoon of low-calorie margarine contains about:
51 calories
70 mg sodium
6 g fat
0 protein
0 carbohydrate
0 cholesterol

Each tablespoon of low-calorie unsalted margarine contains about:
51 calories
1 mg sodium
6 g fat
0 protein
0 carbohydrate
0 cholesterol

LOW-CALORIE BUTTER

Substitute unsalted butter for margarine in the preceding recipe.

Each tablespoon contains about:
51 calories
1 mg sodium
6 g fat
0 protein
0 carbohydrate
18 mg cholesterol

CHOLESTEROL-FREE EGG SUBSTITUTE

1 pinch saffron threads
¼ cup nonfat milk
1 tablespoon nonfat milk powder
1 teaspoon vegetable oil
3 egg whites

Crush the saffron threads to a powder wi th the back of a spoon. Add the milk and stir to dissolve saffron. Add the nonfat milk powder and vegetable oil. Beat the egg whites lightly with a fork. Add milk mixture to egg whites and beat until well blended. Cover and store in the refrigerator for up to 3 days. Stir well before using. Makes 6 tablespoons.

NOTE: A dash of egg yolk may be substituted for the saffron. Three tablespoons (1½ ounces) of egg substitute equals 1 egg.

Each 3-tablespoon serving contains about:
61 calories
102 mg sodium
2 g fat
6 g protein
3 g carbohydrate
1 mg cholesterol

Small Secrets for Great Desserts

The presentation of a dessert is very important if it is to please the eye as well as the palate, and the equipment "makes" the dessert if it is wisely chosen. The following information will reassure even the least experienced of cooks and give them some secrets for success.

Tart or Flan Tins

Choose nonstick tins with a loose base. This will eliminate the need to grease them, which will avoid extra calories and allow for easy turning out of the finished dessert. Fluted-edged tins will make for a more attractive flan or tart. There are old-fashioned flan dishes in ovenproof porcelain that are suitable to serve from, flan rings that allow flans to be made directly on nonstick baking sheets, and, last of all, small, individual tartlet tins that are either round or heart or boat shaped. It is useful to have a few different sizes. Sizes range from one-half inch to about ten inches in diameter. I suggest you use a six-inch tin to serve four and a nine-inch tin to serve six.

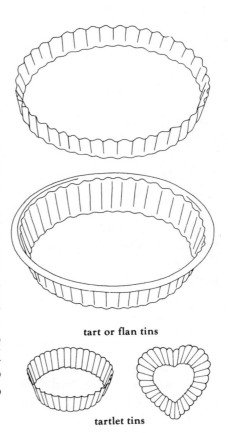

tart or flan tins

tartlet tins

Cake Tins

Cake tins come in a variety of shapes—round, square, and oblong. Normally they are smooth sided, but they are also available fluted, and range in size from six to twelve inches in diameter. A round tin gives the best baking results because the edges are equidistant from the center. It is best to choose a tin with a nonstick aluminum finish to make turning out easy and to eliminate extra calories contributed by greasing.

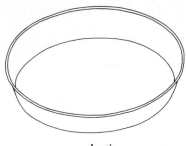

cake tin

Savarin, Baba, and Crown Molds

These molds have a large boss (protuberance) in the center and are used for making flans, puddings, bombes, molded creams, and savarins. They are advantageous for two reasons: they allow for a beautiful presentation because they permit a fruit or cream filling to be placed in the center, and, secondly, ease of cooking. The dough or cream will not be very thick and will cook or set more evenly and quickly in this type of mold. Choose a mold with a nonstick aluminum finish. These molds are available in a variety of sizes.

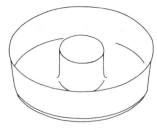

savarin mold

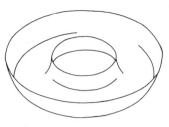

baba mold

Spring-Form Pans

Spring-form pans come in various sizes and are ideal for making mousses, cheesecakes, and ice cream cakes. Removal of the spring-form ring allows for easy turning out.

Soufflé Dishes

These dishes, which come in a wide range of sizes, give the best results when making a soufflé. To serve six, use a one-quart or one-and-one-half-quart soufflé dish. To serve one, use a half-cup size.

Basic Equipment

Spatulas and wooden spoons: Avoid using the same spatulas and wooden spoons for preparing other dishes, a practice that can leave them with a flavor residue incompatible with dessert making.

Hand whisk: Use to thoroughly beat a mixture and to make smooth sauces and creams.

Pastry brush: Use to glaze fruit tarts and pastries.

Rolling pin: Choose one made of hardwood, beech, or boxwood.

Pastry or piping bag and tips: Use to give an attractive finish to desserts, and to make meringue shells, cream puffs, and éclairs.

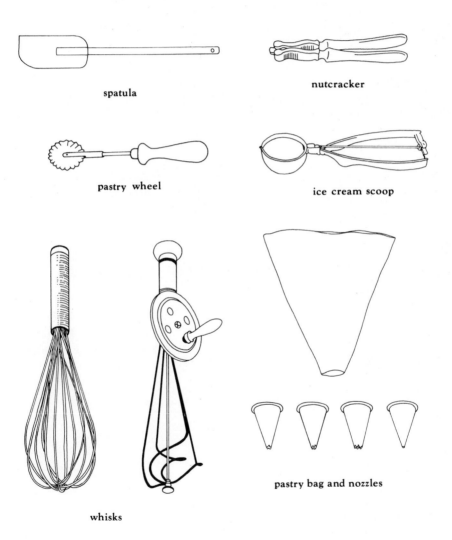

spatula

nutcracker

pastry wheel

ice cream scoop

whisks

pastry bag and nozzles

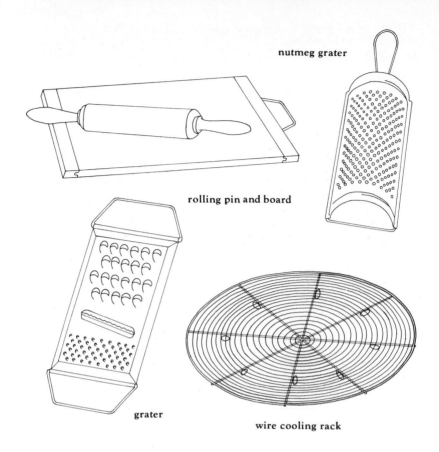

nutmeg grater

rolling pin and board

grater

wire cooling rack

Care of Equipment

Always wash your equipment carefully and dry it well. Avoid using scouring pads as they can damage the finish. Never cut a tart or cake in the tin as this will leave scratches that will make the next dessert stick. Finally, wrap tins and molds in paper before storing to keep them free from rust.

Calorie-, Salt-, Fat-, and Cholesterol-Saving Tips

These tips will help you substitute ingredients low in fats, calories, cholesterol, and salt content for many ingredients in your own favorite recipes. By following these suggestions, you can successfully modify all your recipes. To some degree, recipe modification calls for experimentation. Be daring with ingredient substitutions. You will be amazed at how creative you can be.

Chocolate

Use unsweetened cocoa powder instead of unsweetened chocolate to reduce calories and saturated fat. For each square (1 ounce) of chocolate, use 3 tablespoons cocoa plus 1 tablespoon low-calorie margarine. Place over hot water in the top pan of a double boiler and cook, stirring until smooth. To make semisweet chocolate, add 2 teaspoons fructose to the above. Carob (chips or powder) contains no saturated fat and fewer calories than chocolate because its mild flavor requires less sweetening than chocolate. You can substitute carob in any recipe calling for chocolate. See Rich Carob or Chocolate Ice Cream (page 122) or Chocolate Moussettes (page 57).

Eggs

Egg substitute (commercial or made with the recipe on page 150) can be used in place of eggs in any recipe calling for eggs to lower calories and eliminate cholesterol. If using commercial egg substitute, check labels for calorie and sodium content. Use 3 tablespoons (1½ ounces) egg substitute for each egg.

Egg Whites

Beaten egg whites are the calorie, cholesterol, and salt watcher's dream come true. They add "creamy" volume to desserts. See Lemon Cheesecake (page 110), Heavenly Meringue Tart (page 87), or Chocolate Mousse (page 58).

Fat

Calories, sodium, cholesterol, and fat can be reduced by using low-calorie margarine (commercial or made with the recipe on page 149). See Tart Pastry (page 60). To lower sodium content further, use unsalted margarine. Low-calorie margarine is essentially water whipped with margarine, which saves you 50 calories per tablespoon. Use nonstick cooking equipment and utensils to lower calories and fat content further.

Milk and Dairy Products

Use nonfat milk in recipes that call for milk, nonfat evaporated milk in recipes that call for cream, and low-fat yogurt or low-fat ricotta or cottage cheese in recipes that call for sour cream, cream cheese, or custard sauces, Not only are they lower in calories, cholesterol, and fat, but they are also loaded with nutrients. See French Vanilla Ice Cream (page 121), Strawberry Tart (page 65), Cold Pumpkin Soufflé (page 30), or Lemon Cheesecake (page 110).

Salt

Those on extreme low-sodium diets should use low-sodium baking powder (commercial or made with the formula on page 164). Make it a practice to leave out salt whenever it is called for in a dessert recipe. There is probably not a single dessert in any cookbook that cannot be made successfully without salt.

Sauces and Creams

Use Light Whipped Topping (page 145) instead of whipped cream to thicken desserts, creams, and sauces. See Bavarian Mocha Cream (page 113), Strawberry Mousse Torte (page 83), Peach Mousse (page 54), or Raspberry Cream Sherbet (page 127).

You will reduce calories if you substitute cornstarch or arrowroot when sauces call for flour, because you need only about half as much of either of them as you would flour.

Sweeteners

Fruits (dried, fresh, or unsweetened canned) have their own natural sweetness. Use fruits and fruit juices to sweeten sauces, for poaching liquid, in cookies, and for glazes. See Glazed Summer- or Winter-Fruit Tartlets (page 63), Poached Pears in Chocolate Sauce (page 17), or Savarin with Blueberries (page 67). Fructose can be substituted for sucrose (table sugar). For each cup of sugar, use ½ to ¾ cup fructose. Fructose is twice as sweet as sugar, therefore you need less. However, in recipes where the success of the product depends on sugar, like meringues, use the same amount of fructose as you would table sugar. Fructose has the same calorie count as sugar, but because fructose is sweeter, you use less.

Special Products

Product	Brand Name	Where Distributed	Comments
CHEESES			
Low-sodium Cheddar cheese	Tillamook, Schreibers	Health food stores	
Cheez-Ola Count Down	Fisher Cheeses	Most supermarkets and health food stores	
Low-fat cottage cheese	Knudsen	Supermarkets	
Low-fat, low-sodium cottage cheese	Edgemar Farms	Supermarkets	
Low-fat ricotta cheese (made from partially skimmed milk)	Frigo	Supermarkets	
Low-sodium Gouda cheese		Hickory Farms	
Hoop cheese	Knudsen	Supermarkets	
CONDIMENTS, etc.			
Low-sodium baking powder	Cellu	Supermarkets and health food stores	
Sweet (unsalted) margarine		Supermarkets	Contains no salt. Follow recipe on page 149 for low-calorie margarine. Use in recipes that call for sweet (unsalted) butter.

Product	Brand Name	Where Distributed	Comments
Low-calorie margarine	Fleischmann's, Mazola, Imperial, Parkay	Supermarkets	The calories are lower because margarine is whipped with water to double the volume.
Imitation sour cream	Penn and Quil, Knudsen	Supermarkets	Contains approximately half the calories of regular sour cream. However, it contains hydrogenated fat.
Low-sugar spreads: Strawberry Apricot Grape Boysenberry Orange marmalade Raspberry	Smuckers, Kerns	Supermarkets	Good flavor. No artificial sweeteners added. Contains half the sugar of regular jam. Refer to Nutrient Counter for specific nutrients.
EGG SUBSTITUTE			
Second Nature	Avoset Food Corporation	Supermarkets	Has half the sodium content of most other egg substitutes.
NUTS			
Unsalted nuts	Planters	Most supermarkets	
Raw nuts		Health food stores	Have no salt or oil added.

Product	Brand Name	Where Distributed	Comments
Peanut butter, nonhydrogenated	Laura Scudder, Ralph's Old-Fashioned, Safeway's Old-Fashioned	Most supermarkets	
Peanut butter, unsalted	Peter Pan	Most supermarkets	

NON-DAIRY LOW-CALORIE WHIPPED TOPPINGS

Product	Brand Name	Where Distributed	Comments
Cool Whip	Bird's Eye	Supermarkets	
Dream Whip		Supermarkets	Contains less calories.
D'Zert Whip	Presto Foods	Supermarkets	
Dieter's Gourmet	Dieter's Gourmet	Supermarkets	Contains no artificial sweeteners. Only 8 calories per tablespoon.

MISCELLANEOUS

Product	Brand Name	Where Distributed	Comments
Carob chips, carob powder		Supermarkets and health food stores	Chocolate-flavored chips or powder milled from the carob-tree pod. Carob is lower in fat than chocolate and sweeter, so you use less sugar. Refer to page 164 for substitutions.
Fructose	Superose	Supermarkets and health food stores	Fructose liquid sweetener is sweeter than ordinary sugar, therefore you may use less and save calories. Helps retain moisture in all baked goods. May cause more browning than sugar, so you may wish to cut baking time by about 10 percent.

Product	Brand Name	Where Distributed	Comments
Fructose	Estee	Supermarkets and health food stores	Fructose in granulated form. Refer to page 164 for more information on fructose.
Fruit nectars	Knudsen	Supermarkets and health food stores	Knudsen's nectars are unfiltered, with no sugar, preservatives, or artificial flavoring or coloring.
	Kern		Kern's nectars contain no artificial flavoring or preservatives. However, sugar is added.
Phyllo dough		Greek or Armenian markets, many delicatessens and some supermarkets	Best if bought fresh. Refer to page 76 for information on phyllo dough.
Carr's Wheatmeal Biscuits	Carr's	Gourmet section of supermarkets	

Table of Substitutions and Equivalents

The table of substitutions and equivalents will help you modify your favorite dessert recipes so that they will be lower in calories, salt, fat, and cholesterol. It contains the conversions for regular and artificial sweeteners according to brand name, as well as a wide variety of other commonly used ingredients.

The use of artificial sweeteners is not encouraged. They are listed for those who are medically advised to use them. Note that in many recipes, such as meringues, they cannot be substituted for fructose or sucrose (table sugar).

According to recent research, a small amount of artificial sweetener may not be harmful. If you consume a large quantity of "diet drinks" or use a lot of artificial sweetener in liquids, you may want to reconsider its use. The Food and Drug Administration (FDA) ruling on saccharin states that additional research is needed to determine whether saccharin is safe for use. The FDA warns, however, that saccharin may cause cancer. The American Diabetes Association does, however, advocate the use of saccharin for diabetics.

There is no type of sugar that is "better" for you. All crystal-type sugars, no matter what their color, have the same caloric count (forty-eight calories per tablespoon), so use them sparingly. Tablespoon for tablespoon, honey contains more calories than sugar, but you need less honey to sweeten a dessert to the same intensity. Honey contains a few needed trace minerals, but not enough and not in great enough amounts to make it nutritious. Honey, like any form of sugar, is an "empty-calorie" food.

Fructose, the natural sugar made from fruits (apples, oranges, pears, bananas) and vegetables, is available in liquid or granulated form. The calorie-lowering effect is worth the additional cost over ordinary sugar if you use it frequently. If used only in small amounts, however, the calorie savings may not be worth the extra expense.

Arrowroot and cornstarch can be substituted for flour. Tablespoon for tablespoon, all three contain the same number of calories (twenty-nine calories per tablespoon), but because less arrowroot or cornstarch than flour is needed to thicken to the same degree, there are fewer calories in the finished recipe. For fruit glazes or syrups, always use cornstarch. It gives them a shiny, smooth appearance.

Eggs are an excellent and economical source of nutrients. For those who must watch cholesterol, egg yolks should be limited. The use of egg substitutes is encouraged to reduce calories and eliminate extra cholesterol. Refer to the recipe on page 150 for the nutrient breakdown of homemade egg substitute, and the Nutrient Counter on page 171 for the nutrient breakdowns of eggs and commercial egg substitutes.

Item	Substitution or Equivalent

Artificial Sweeteners (Sugar Substitutes)

Sugar Twin:
1 teaspoon	=	1 teaspoon sugar

Sugar Twin, Brown:
1 teaspoon	=	1 teaspoon sugar

Sweet 'n Low:
1/10 teaspoon	=	1 teaspoon sugar
1/3 teaspoon	=	1 tablespoon sugar
1 teaspoon	=	1/6 cup sugar
1 1/2 teaspoons	=	1/4 cup sugar
3 teaspoons	=	1/2 cup sugar
6 teaspoons (2 tablespoons)	=	1 cup sugar

Adolph's Sugar Substitute:
2 shakes of jar	=	1 rounded teaspoon sugar
1/4 teaspoon	=	1 tablespoon sugar
1 teaspoon	=	1/4 cup sugar
2 1/2 teaspoons	=	2/3 cup sugar
1 tablespoon	=	3/4 cup sugar
4 teaspoons	=	1 cup sugar

Sucaryl (Liquid Sweetener):
1/8 teaspoon	=	1 teaspoon sugar
1/2 teaspoon	=	4 teaspoons sugar
3/4 teaspoon	=	2 tablespoons sugar
1 1/2 teaspoons	=	1/4 cup sugar
3 teaspoons (1 tablespoon)	=	1/2 cup sugar

Item		Substitution or Equivalent

Fructose

½ teaspoon	=	1 teaspoon sugar
1½ teaspoons	=	1 tablespoon sugar
2 tablespoons	=	¼ cup sugar
¼ cup	=	½ cup sugar
6 tablespoons	=	¾ cup sugar
½ cup	=	1 cup sugar

Baking Powder

1 teaspoon	=	1 teaspoon baking soda + ½ teaspoon cream of tartar

Baking powder, low-sodium

1½ teaspoons	=	½ teaspoon baking powder

Recipe: Your druggist can make low-sodium baking powder for you by using the following formula. This formula yields about 4½ ounces.

Potassium bicarbonate	39.8 grams
Cornstarch	20.0 grams
Tartaric acid	7.5 grams
Potassium bitartrate	56.1 grams

Carob powder

3 tablespoons powder + 2 tablespoons water	=	1 ounce unsweetened chocolate

Chocolate

1 square, 1 ounce	=	4 tablespoons grated

Chocolate, unsweetened

1 ounce	=	3 tablespoons cocoa + 1 tablespoon low-calorie margarine

Chocolate, unsweetened

1 ounce + 2 teaspoons fructose	=	1⅔ ounces semisweet chocolate

Cream, heavy whipping

1 cup	=	2 cups whipped

Item		Substitution or Equivalent

Eggs

1	=	3 tablespoons egg substitute
1 medium egg white	=	1½ tablespoons
9 medium egg whites	=	1 cup
1 egg yolk	=	1 tablespoon
1 egg yolk	=	1 tablespoon egg substitute

Flours (for thickening)

1 tablespoon	=	1½ teaspoons cornstarch or arrowroot

Fruits

Apples, 1 pound, 4 small	=	3 cups sliced or chopped
Apricots, 1 pound, 6 to 8	=	2 cups chopped
Bananas, 1 pound, 4 medium	=	2 cups mashed
Berries, 1 pint	=	2 cups
Cantaloupe, 2 pounds	=	3 cups diced
Grapes, Concord, ¼ pound, 30	=	1 cup
Grapes, Thompson seedless, ¼ pound, 40	=	1 cup
Honeydew melon, 2 pounds	=	3 cups diced
Lemon, 1	=	1 to 3 tablespoons juice 1 to 1½ teaspoons grated zest
Mangoes, 1 pound, 2 average	=	1½ cups chopped
Nectarines, 1 pound, 3 average	=	2 cups chopped
Orange, 1 medium	=	6 to 8 tablespoons juice 1 tablespoon grated zest ¾ cup sectioned
Peaches, 1 pound, 4 medium	=	2 cups sliced or chopped
Pears, 1 pound, 4 medium	=	2 cups sliced or chopped
Pineapple, 3 pounds, 1 medium	=	2½ cups chopped
Prunes, 1 pound, cooked and drained	=	2 cups

Item		Substitution or Equivalent
Tangerines, 1 pound, 4 average	=	2 cups sectioned
Watermelon, 10 to 12 pounds, 1 average	=	20 to 24 cups cubed
Gelatin		
1 envelope (¼ ounce)	=	1 tablespoon
Honey		
1 cup	=	1¼ cups sugar + ¼ cup liquid
Margarine		
1 cube (¼ pound)	=	½ cup or 8 tablespoons
Milk, nonfat evaporated, chilled, 1 cup	=	2 cups whipped
Nuts, shelled		
Almonds, ½ pound	=	2 cups
Almonds, 42 chopped	=	½ cup
Almonds, 4 ounces, blanched, slivered	=	1 cup
Brazil nuts, ½ pound	=	1½ cups
Peanuts, ½ pound	=	1 cup
Pecans, ½ pound	=	2 cups
Pistachios, 1 pound	=	3⅔ cups
Walnuts, ½ pound	=	2 cups
Walnuts, 15 chopped	=	½ cup
Yeast		
Active dry, 1 package	=	1 tablespoon
Compressed, 1 cake	=	1 package active dry
Yogurt		
plain, 1 cup	=	1 cup buttermilk

Metric Conversion Tables

Flour, Fructose, and Sugar Measurements

To measure flour, spoon it into a cup and, with the edge of a knife blade, level it off even with the cup lip.

Flour measurements	Ounces	Nearest equivalents
1 tb	¼ oz	7½ g
¼ c; 4 tb	1¼ oz	35 g
⅓ c; 5 tb	1½ oz	50 g
½ c	2½ oz	70 g
⅔ c	3¼ oz	100 g
¾ c	3½ oz	105 g
1 c	5 oz	140 g
1¼ c	6 oz	175 g
1⅓ c	6½ oz	190 g
1½ c	7½ oz	215 g
2 c	10 oz	285 g
3½ c	16 oz; 1 lb	454 g
3¾ c	17½ oz	500 g

Sugar measurements	Ounces	Nearest equivalents
1 tsp	⅙ oz	5 g
1 tb	½ oz	12-15 g
¼ c; 4 tb	1¾ oz	50 g
⅓ c; 5 tb	2¼ oz	65 g
½ c	3½ oz	100 g
⅔ c	4½ oz	125 g
¾ c	5 oz	145 g
1 c	7 oz (6¾ oz)	190-200 g
1¼ c	8½ oz	240 g
1⅓ c	9 oz	245 g
1½ c	9½ oz	275 g
1⅔ c	11 oz	325 g
1¾ c	11¾ oz	240 g
2 c	13½ oz	380-400 g

Liquid Measure Conversions

Cups and spoons	Liquid ounces	Approximate metric term	Approximate centiliters	Actual milliliters
1 tsp	⅙ oz	1 tsp	½ cl	5 ml
1 tb	½ oz	1 tb	1½ cl	15 ml
¼ c; 4 tb	2 oz	½ dl; 4 tb	6 cl	59 ml
⅓ c; 5 tb	2⅔ oz	¾ dl; 5 tb	8 cl	79 ml
½ c	4 oz	1 dl	12 cl	119 ml
⅔ c	5⅓ oz	1½ dl	15 cl	157 ml
¾ c	6 oz	1¾ dl	18 cl	178 ml
1 c	8 oz	¼ l	24 cl	237 ml
1¼ c	10 oz	3 dl	30 cl	296 ml
1⅓ c	10⅔ oz	3¼ dl	33 cl	325 ml
1½ c	12 oz	3½ dl	35 cl	355 ml
1⅔ c	13⅓	3¾ dl	39 cl	385 ml
1¾ c	14 oz	4 dl	41 cl	414 ml
2 c; 1 pt	16 oz	½ l	47 cl	473 ml
2½ c	20 oz	6 dl	60 cl	592 ml
3 c	24 oz	¾ l	70 cl	710 ml
3½ c	28 oz	⅘ l; 8 dl	83 cl	829 ml
4 c; 1 qt	32 oz	1 l	95 cl	946 ml
5 c	40 oz	1¼ l	113 cl	1134 ml
6 c; 1½ qt	48 oz	1½ l	142 cl	1420 ml
8 c; 2 qt	64 oz	2 l	190 cl	1893 ml
10 c; 2½ qt	80 oz	2½ l	235 cl	2366 ml
12 c; 3 qt	96 oz	2¾ l	284 cl	2839 ml
4 qt	128 oz	3¾ l	375 cl	3785 ml
5 qt		4¾ l		
6 qt		5½ l (or 6 l)		
8 qt		7½ l (or 8 l)		

To convert
Ounces to milliliters: Multiply ounces by 29.57
Quarts to liters: Multiply quarts by 0.95
Milliliters to ounces: Multiply milliliters by 0.034
Liters to quarts: Multiply liters by 1.057

Ounces to Grams

Ounces	Convenient equivalent	Actual weight
1 oz	30 g	28.35 g
2 oz	60 g	56.7 g
3 oz	85 g	85.05 g
4 oz	115 g	113.4 g
5 oz	140 g	141.8 g
6 oz	180 g	170.1 g
8 oz	225 g	226.8 g
9 oz	250 g	255.2 g
10 oz	285 g	283.5 g
12 oz	340 g	340.2 g
14 oz	400 g	396.9 g
16 oz	450 g	453.6 g
20 oz	560 g	566.99 g
24 oz	675 g	680.4 g

To convert
Ounces to grams: Multiply ounces by 28.35
Grams to ounces: Multiply grams by 0.035

Selected Measurements

Low-Calorie Margarine, Margarine, or Butter

1 teaspoon	=	⅙ ounce	or 5 grams
1 tablespoon	=	½ ounce	or 15 grams
½ cup (1 stick)	=	4 ounces	or 115 grams
1 cup (2 sticks)	=	8 ounces	or 230 grams
2 cups (4 sticks)	=	1 pound	or 454 grams

Nuts (chopped)
1 cup	=	5 ounces	or 155 grams

Pounds to Grams and Kilograms

Pounds	Convenient equivalent	Actual weight
¼ lb	115 g	113.4 g
½ lb	225 g	226.8 g
¾ lb	340 g	340.2 g
1 lb	450 g	453.6 g
1¼ lb	565 g	566.99 g
1½ lb	675 g	680.4 g
1¾ lb	800 g	794 g
2 lb	900 g	908 g
2½ lb	1125 g	1134 g
3 lb	1350 g	1360 g
3½ lb	1500 g	1588 g
4 lb	1800 g	1814 g
4½ lb	2 kg	2041 g
5 lb	2¼ kg	2268 g
5½ lb	2½ kg	2495 g
6 lb	2¾ kg	2727 g
7 lb	3¼ kg	3175 g
8 lb	3½ kg	3629 g
9 lb	4 kg	4028 g
10 lb	4½ kg	4536 g
12 lb	5½ kg	5443 g
14 lb	6¼ kg	6350 g
15 lb	6¾ kg	6804 g
16 lb	7¼ kg	7258 g
18 lb	8 kg	8165 g
20 lb	9 kg	9072 g
25 lb	11¼ kg	11,340 g

Nutrient Counter

The calorie, sodium, fat, protein, carbohydrate, and cholesterol contents of foods used in *Light Desserts* are listed here for commonly used portions. This information is invaluable in recipe modification.

Figures shown represent average nutrient values. (These references include standard error of the mean.) A dash indicates figures not available; "tr" (trace) is used for figures less than 1.

Food and Description	Measure or Quantity	Calories	Sodium mg	Fat g	Protein g	Carbohydrate g	Cholesterol mg
A							
Alcoholic beverages							
distilled							
gin, rum, vodka, whiskey	1 ounce	75	tr	0	0	0	0
brandy	1 ounce	73	tr	0	0	0	0
cognac	1 ounce	73	tr	0	0	0	0
liqueurs							
cordial-anisette	1 ounce	105	tr	0	0	10	0
apricot brandy	1 ounce	91	tr	0	0	8	0
Benedictine	1 ounce	100	tr	0	0	9	0
Crème de Menthe	1 ounce	94	tr	0	0	8	0
Curaçao	1 ounce	77	tr	0	0	8	0
Cointreau	1 ounce	85	tr	0	0	9	0
Grand Marnier	1 ounce	93	tr	0	0	8	0
Kahlúa	1 ounce	83	tr	0	0	9	0
Crème de Cacao	1 ounce	101	tr	0	0	14	0
orange liqueur	1 ounce	90	tr	0	0	8	0
coffee liqueur	1 ounce	92	tr	0	0	8	0
Kirsch	1 ounce	83	tr	0	0	9	0
wine							
port	3½ ounces	158	4	0	tr	14	0
dry sherry	2 ounces	84	2	0	tr	5	0

Food and Description	Measure or Quantity	Calories	Sodium mg	Fat g	Protein g	Carbohydrate g	Cholesterol mg
champagne, extra dry	3 ounces	63	0	0	tr	2	0
Dubonnet	3 ounces	96	tr	0	0	—	0
Madeira	3 ounces	105	tr	0	tr	1	0
dry marsala	3 ounces	124	tr	0	tr	—	0
sweet marsala	3 ounces	182	tr	0	tr	—	0
muscatel	4 ounces	190	4	0	tr	14	0
dry red wine	3 ounces	85	5	0	tr	4	0
sake	3 ounces	75	—	0	—	—	0
dry vermouth	3½ ounces	112	—	0	—	1	0
sweet vermouth	3½ ounces	151	—	0	—	12	0
dry white wine	3 ounces	85	tr	0	tr	4	0
Almonds, raw unsalted	6 tablespoons chopped	547	3	54	19	20	0
	½ cup chopped ground slivered flaked	360	2	36	12	12	0
Apple, fresh	1 medium	80	1	1	tr	22	0
dried	¼ cup	60	4	1	1	61	0
Apple juice, unsweetened	½ cup	60	4	tr	tr	15	0
Apricots, fresh	1 medium	25	tr	tr	tr	13	0
dried	¼ cup	65	7	tr	1	15	0
Apricot jelly							
low calorie	1 tablespoon	26	tr	0	0	8	0
regular	1 tablespoon	51	2	0	tr	13	0
low-sugar spread	1 tablespoon	8	tr	0	tr	2	0
Arrowroot	1 tablespoon	29	4	0	0	7	0

B

Food and Description	Measure or Quantity	Calories	Sodium mg	Fat g	Protein g	Carbohydrate g	Cholesterol mg
Baking powder							
low sodium	1 teaspoon	5	tr	0	0	1	0
regular	1 teaspoon	4	247	0	0	1	0
Baking soda	1 teaspoon	0	821	0	0	0	0
Banana	1 medium	127	2	tr	2	33	0

Food and Description	Measure or Quantity	Calories	Sodium mg	Fat g	Protein g	Carbohydrate g	Cholesterol mg
Blackberries							
fresh	½ cup	42	tr	1	1	9	0
frozen, unsweetened	4 ounces	54	1	tr	1	12	0
Blueberries							
fresh	½ cup	43	tr	tr	tr	10	0
frozen, unsweetened	4 ounces	66	1	tr	1	16	0
Brazil nuts	10	240	tr	25	5	4	0
Brown sugar substitute	1 tablespoon	12	18	0	0	3	0
regular	1 tablespoon	52	3	0	0	13	0
Butter							
salted	1 tablespoon	108	124	12	tr	tr	33
unsalted	1 tablespoon	107	1	12	tr	tr	39

C

Food and Description	Measure or Quantity	Calories	Sodium mg	Fat g	Protein g	Carbohydrate g	Cholesterol mg
Cantaloupe, fresh	¼ of 5" melon	30	12	tr	tr	7	0
Carob, chips	½ cup (3 ounces)	112	8	1	2	48	—
powder, unsweetened	1 tablespoon	14	1	tr	tr	6	—
Cashews, unsalted	10 nuts	100	2	8	3	5	0
dry roasted	½ cup chopped	280	7	23	9	15	0
	ground	300	8	25	10	17	0
Cheese (page 179)							
Cherries, fresh	10	35	1	tr	tr	8	0
canned, unsweetened	½ cup	43	2	tr	tr	11	0
Chocolate,							
semisweet	1 ounce (1 square)	147	64	8	2	17	tr
chips	1 ounce	124	4	7	1	19	tr
Cocoa	1 tablespoon	27	27	tr	tr	5	0
chocolate wafer	1 wafer	20	29	1	tr	—	0
Coconut							
shredded, unsweetened	1 tablespoon	22	1	2	tr	1	0
Cornstarch	1 tablespoon	36	—	tr	tr	9	0
Cranberry juice	½ cup	24	5	—	—	6	0
Cran-grape juice	½ cup	72	5	—	—	16	0

Food and Description	Measure or Quantity	Calories	Sodium mg	Fat g	Protein g	Carbohydrate g	Cholesterol mg
Cream cheese	1 tablespoon	50	42	5	1	tr	17
	8 ounces	800	672	80	16	13	272
Currants	1 tablespoon	8	tr	tr	tr	tr	0
	¼ cup	32	2	tr	tr	8	0
D							
Dates	10	274	1	tr	2	73	0
	½ cup chopped	244	1	tr	2	65	0
E							
Egg substitute	1½ ounces	40	85	1	4	4	0
Egg, white only	1 medium	16	47	tr	3	tr	0
Egg, whole	1 medium	78	59	5	6	tr	264
F							
Filberts	10	97	tr	10	2	3	0
	½ cup chopped	400	1	40	8	12	0
	ground	440	1	44	9	13	0
Flour							
all purpose	1 tablespoon	29	tr	tr	tr	6	0
whole wheat	1 tablespoon	25	tr	tr	1	5	0
whole wheat or all purpose	1 cup	400	4	2	16	85	0
Fructose	1 tablespoon	46	tr	0	0	12	0
G							
Gelatin, unflavored	1 envelope	23	8	tr	6	0	0
Graham cracker	1 cracker	27	47	tr	tr	5	0
Grapefruit, fresh	½ medium	41	1	tr	tr	11	0
canned, unsweetened	½ cup	30	4	tr	tr	8	0

Food and Description	Measure or Quantity	Calories	Sodium mg	Fat g	Protein g	Carbohydrate g	Cholesterol mg
Grape jelly							
low calorie	1 tablespoon	7	tr	0	0	2	0
regular	1 tablespoon	55	3	tr	tr	14	0
low-sugar spread	1 tablespoon	8	tr	0	tr	2	0
Grape juice	½ cup	80	2	tr	tr	20	0
white grape juice	½ cup	80	2	tr	tr	20	0
H							
Hazelnuts	10	97	tr	10	2	3	0
	½ cup ground	440	1	44	9	13	0
	chopped	400	1	40	8	12	0
Honey	1 tablespoon	61	1	0	tr	16	0
Honeydew melon	¼ of 5" melon	33	12	tr	tr	8	0
K							
Kiwi	1 medium	30	tr	tr	tr	7	0
L							
Lemon juice	1 tablespoon	4	tr	tr	tr	1	0
Liqueurs (page 171)	¼ cup	16	tr	tr	tr	4	0
M							
Mandarin orange canned, unsweetened	½ cup	30	3	tr	tr	8	0
Mango, fresh	1 medium	130	14	1	1	17	0
Maple syrup low calorie	1 tablespoon	9	--	0	0	2	0

Food and Description	Measure or Quantity	Calories	Sodium mg	Fat g	Protein g	Carbohydrate g	Cholesterol mg
regular	1 tablespoon	50	3	0	0	13	0
Margarine							
low calorie	1 tablespoon	50	95	6	-	-	0
regular	1 tablespoon	100	109	11	-	-	0
unsalted	1 tablespoon	100	1	11	-	-	0
Marmalade							
low calorie	1 tablespoon	21	0	-	-	5	-
regular	1 tablespoon	54	8	0	tr	14	0
low-sugar spread	1 tablespoon	8	tr	0	tr	2	0
Milk							
buttermilk	1 cup	92	212	2	8	10	10
evaporated nonfat	½ cup	92	140	tr	9	14	8
nonfat	1 cup	89	128	tr	8	12	5
whole	1 cup	150	120	8	8	12	34
low fat (2%)	1 cup	122	122	5	8	12	20
N							
Nectars							
unsweetened	½ cup	23	tr	0	0	8	0
sweetened	½ cup	75	tr	0	0	18	0
O							
Orange	1 medium	71	1	tr	2	18	0
Orange juice, unsweetened	½ cup	60	1	tr	1	13	0
P							
Papaya, fresh	½	40	3	tr	tr	10	0
Pecans, unsalted	12 halves	104	tr	11	1	2	0
	½ cup chopped	416	tr	44	4	8	0
	ground	450	tr	48	4	9	0
Peaches							
fresh	1 medium	38	1	tr	tr	10	0

Food and Description	Measure or Quantity	Calories	Sodium mg	Fat g	Protein g	Carbohydrate g	Cholesterol mg
canned, unsweetened	½ cup	31	2	tr	tr	8	0
frozen, unsweetened	½ cup	35	2	tr	tr	8	0
Phyllo dough	1 sheet	52	tr	tr	tr	13	0
Pineapple juice, unsweetened	½ cup	64	tr	tr	tr	16	0
Pineapple							
fresh	1 slice	44	1	tr	tr	11	0
canned, unsweetened	1 slice	39	1	tr	tr	10	0
crushed	½ cup	35	1	tr	tr	7	0
Pistachio nuts, shelled	10 nuts	29	—	3	1	1	0
	1 tablespoon ground	15	—	2	tr	tr	0
	½ cup ground	132	—	13	4	4	0
	chopped	120	—	12	4	4	0
Prunes, dried	5	215	7	tr	2	57	0
Pumpkin, canned, unsalted	½ cup	40	2	tr	1	9	0
R							
Raisins	1 tablespoon	29	3	tr	tr	8	0
Raspberries							
fresh	½ cup	38	tr	tr	tr	9	0
canned water-pack	½ cup	35	1	tr	tr	9	0
frozen, unsweetened	½ cup	36	1	t	t	9	0
S							
Safflower oil	1 tablespoon	124	0	14	0	0	0
Salt	1 teaspoon	—	1955	0	0	0	0
Sesame seeds	1 tablespoon	87	—	8	3	3	0
Sesame seed oil	1 tablespoon	126	0	14	0	0	0
Sour cream							
low calorie	1 tablespoon	15	—	—	—	—	—
regular	1 tablespoon	26	6	3	tr	tr	17
Strawberries							
fresh	10	37	1	tr	tr	8	0
frozen, unsweetened	4 ounces	40	3	tr	tr	10	0

Food and Description	Measure or Quantity	Calories	Sodium mg	Fat g	Protein g	Carbohydrate g	Cholesterol mg
jelly							
low calorie	1 tablespoon	26	tr	0	0	7	0
regular	1 tablespoon	51	2	0	tr	13	0
low-sugar spread	1 tablespoon	8	tr	0	tr	2	0
Sugar	1 tablespoon	46	tr	0	0	12	0
Sugar substitutes	1 packet	4	0	0	0	1	0
T							
Tangerine	1 medium	35	1	tr	tr	11	0
V							
Vanilla wafers	1 wafer	17	9	tr	tr	3	-
W							
Walnuts, raw	10	98	tr	10	2	2	0
unsalted	1 tablespoon ground	50	tr	5	1	1	0
	½ cup ground	440	3	20	8	8	0
	chopped	400	3	22	9	9	0
Watermelon	½ cup	26	1	tr	tr	6	0
Wheatmeal Biscuits (Carr's)	1 biscuit	16	22	tr	tr	3	-
Wine (page 171)							
Y							
Yogurt, low fat							
fruit flavored	1 cup	231	133	2	10	43	14
plain	1 cup	143	159	3	12	16	10
Z							
Zwieback crackers	1 cracker	31	18	tr	tr	5	-

NUTRIENT COUNTER FOR CHEESES

Note: All quantities are 1 ounce unless otherwise indicated.

Cheese	Calories	Sodium mg	Cholesterol mg	Fat in Grams Total	Saturated	Unsaturated
Blue	100	396	21	8.15	5.30	2.85
Brick	105	159	27	8.41	5.32	3.09
Brie	95	178	28	7.85	–	–
Camembert	85	239	20	6.88	4.33	2.55
Cheddar	114	176	30	9.40	5.98	3.42
Colby	112	171	27	9.10	5.73	3.37
Cottage, creamed (1 cup)	217	850	31	9.47	5.99	3.48
Cottage, 2% low fat (1 cup)	203	918	10	2.30	1.46	.84
Cottage, 1% low fat (1 cup)	164	918	10	2.30	1.46	.84
Cottage, dry curd (1 cup)	123	19	10	.61	.40	.21
Cream Cheese	99	84	31	9.89	6.23	3.66
Edam	101	274	25	7.88	4.98	2.90
Feta	75	316	25	6.03	4.24	1.79
Gouda	101	232	32	7.78	4.99	2.79
Gruyère	117	95	31	9.17	5.36	3.81
Limburger	93	227	26	7.72	4.75	2.97
Monterey Jack	106	152	–	8.58	–	–
Mozzarella, part skim	80	106	22	6.12	3.73	2.39
Muenster	104	178	27	8.52	5.42	3.10
Parmesan, grated (1 tablespoon)	129	528	22	8.51	5.41	3.10
	31	88	–	1.7	–	–
Provolone	100	248	20	7.55	4.82	2.73
Ricotta, whole milk (1 cup)	428	207	124	31.93	20.41	11.52
Ricotta, part skim milk (1 cup)	340	307	76	19.46	12.12	7.34
Romano	110	340	29	7.64	–	–
Swiss	107	74	26	7.78	5.04	2.74

Cheese	Calories	Sodium mg	Cholesterol mg	Fat in Grams		
				Total	Saturated	Unsaturated
Pasteurized Process						
American	106	406	27	8.86	5.58	3.28
Swiss	95	388	24	7.09	4.55	2.54
Swiss Cheese Food	92	440	23	6.84	--	--
American Cheese Spread	82	381	16	6.02	3.78	2.24
Low-Sodium Cheeses						
American	110	10	--	9	--	--
Gouda	110	10	--	9	--	--

Courtesy of the United States Department of Agriculture, *Composition of Foods*, Agricultural Handbook No. 8, 1963.

Recipe Index

182   Light Desserts